THE GUIDE TO FAMILY LAW

The
Guide to
Family Law

MALCOLM C. KRONBY

PaperJacks

A division of General Publishing Co. Limited
Don Mills, Ontario

ISBN 0-88770-159-0

PaperJacks, A Division of General Publishing Co. Ltd.,
30 Lesmill Road, Don Mills,
Ontario, M3B 2T6

Design/Peter Maher
Manufactured in Canada

Contents

Introduction

What's a "legal separation"?

Doesn't the mother always get custody of the children?

How do you *prove* adultery?

In my practice, which is mostly in the field of family law, I've been asked these questions and others like them hundreds of times.

Most laymen who attempt to achieve an understanding of family law are burdened by myth and confused by misconception. They hear third-hand and usually exaggerated stories of the complexity and cost of divorce proceedings. They are intimidated by the prospect of having to appear in court, and put off by technical legal language.

That's why this book was written — to explain in simple language the rights, obligations and remedies of family law.

Well, what is family law?

It's the entire range of statutes, regulations and precedents that govern the relations between husband and wife and between parents and children. This includes the body of law on marriage, divorce and annulment, on custody of children, and property rights within the family. This vast and complex field of law touches the lives of all of us.

The law relating to formation and solemnization of marriage is contained in provincial statutes, which are roughly the same all across the country. The Divorce Act is a federal statute, so that there is, thankfully, only one such enactment for the whole of Canada. However, the regulations governing the procedure of getting a divorce properly before the court vary somewhat from province to province.

The law concerning the custody of children is partly contained in provincial statutes and regulations, which are pretty similar from Newfoundland to British Columbia. The Divorce Act also has sections dealing with custody of children, but these are only applicable in connection with divorce proceedings. As we'll see, the Divorce Act states that custody orders and other orders for "corollary relief" — the things that may go along with a divorce, such as custody, support payments and visiting rights — should be nation-wide in scope and effect; but, probably because there is a large body of older provincial law in these areas, it doesn't seem to work out that way.

When the present Divorce Act came into force in July 1968, it created grounds for divorce that had never previously existed in Canada. For practical purposes, prior to July 1968, the only ground for divorce was adultery. (If you lived in Quebec or Newfoundland there was no way to get a divorce under provincial procedures; a petition had to be presented to the federal Senate to pass a statute dissolving the marriage.) These restricted grounds created many cases of hardship. For example, a husband and wife might have been separated for ten years, in which time the husband might be living with another woman by whom he had children, but there couldn't be a divorce unless his estranged wife saw fit to sue him on the ground of his obvious adultery. Frequently she wouldn't do it, simply out of spite. In other cases, a wife might be the victim of sadistic cruelty, but she couldn't get a divorce unless her husband committed adultery. Many marriages were destroyed by incurable insanity of one of the parties, but the other had no hope of divorce in the absence of adultery.

The Divorce Act (1968) created grounds of cruelty and marriage breakdown (meaning, roughly, separation for a specified period) to go along with adultery. Other grounds were established as well but, as we'll see, these rarely arise in actual practice. Probably the grounds of adultery, cruelty and separation cover 99 per cent of the cases that now come to court. But divorce *is* still a complex business (which is not to say it should be that way), despite the claims of those who sell do-it-yourself divorce kits or offer so-called divorce aid services with supposedly guaranteed results. Personally I think anyone who is involved in a divorce, and who fails to get the best legal representation available, is like a patient doing his own surgery. He might be lucky enough to survive.

I've tried to make the information in this book as

accurate as my knowledge and the state of the law will permit. But laws change. Statutes are amended, appeal courts overturn long-standing precedents, and, especially, circumstances alter results. Often a fine factual distinction between two cases produces two totally different judgments.

It seems to me that no field of law is in such a state of flux as is family law. Hardly a week has gone by since the Divorce Act was passed without a significant new decision being reported. Yet, many facets of divorce law remain unsettled and controversial. That's one reason why family law is so interesting and challenging.

A second reason is the emotional load carried by so many cases. Two businessmen can sue each other for a million dollars but have lunch together during a break in the trial. Parents fighting over the custody of a child literally want to destroy each other.

There's a third reason why this field of law is fascinating. Many cases in family law are what I would call "hinge points" in the lives of the parties. The course of a lifetime can be determined by the judgment in a divorce case; it's even more obviously so in a child-custody case.

A word of caution: if separation or divorce or child custody is your problem, go to a lawyer. This book is no substitute for the working relationship between lawyer and client, nor can it possibly give you legal advice. In presenting a general survey of family law in Canada, it's quite impossible to deal with every aspect, or to make the precise factual distinctions that can utterly alter a judgment in a given case. My hope is that this book may help you to understand and face a problem, and so work more effectively with your lawyer, the only person qualified to advise and represent you.

On page 132 you will find an appendix, "What Your Lawyer Will Probably Want to Know", which is intended to save you and your lawyer time and effort in the first interview.

This book has been written for the most part from the point of view of a lawyer practising in Ontario. The author doesn't pretend to be intimately familiar with the statutes of each province. Although the broad principles of family law are similar all across Canada, differences are often hidden in the interstices of statute law. Where reference is made to a provincial statute, it will be an Ontario statute unless otherwise stated. At the end of this book there is a comparative table of statutes for all the provinces, the better to assist you in consulting the statute applicable to your situation in your province.

M.C.K.
Toronto
August 1972

1
The Legal
Remedies Available

At the outset of this book, the reader should be aware that a variety of alternative remedies is available in matrimonial disputes. In order of severity or finality, they are:

(a) A separation agreement or, in provinces other than Ontario, a decree of judicial separation (dealt with in Chapter 3).

(b) Proceedings by the wife in "Family Court" for support for herself and her children, and, if support is awarded, custody of the children. If a separation agreement already exists, and the husband isn't in breach of its terms, that's a complete defence on his part to the Family Court action. (See Chapter 4.)

(c) An application by either parent for custody of the children, with or without maintenance (child support), subject to the awarding (or refusing) of visiting rights of the other parent. The court always has the power to look at arrangements for the children, even if there's a separation agreement, or previous custody, maintenance or access orders. (See Chapter 5.)

(d) A lawsuit for alimony, with or without a claim (or husband's counter-claim) for child custody and maintenance. Alimony is a money award to the wife; the husband can never sue for alimony.

A valid, subsisting separation agreement is a complete defence to a claim for alimony, but if the husband is in breach of the separation agreement, the wife has every right to sue. (See Chapter 6.)

(e) A petition for divorce, with or without claims for maintenance for the wife, custody of the children and/or maintenance for them. The husband can also turn it around and, in the context of a divorce, claim maintenance for himself payable by the wife, and custody of the children and/or maintenance for them.

You don't need a separation agreement to petition for divorce. Also, if you have a separation agreement, the court can disregard its terms when considering the divorce petition, although this rarely happens. (See Chapter 7.)

Also discussed in this book are annulment of marriage (Chapter 8), property rights (Chapter 9) and, of course, marriage itself, in the next chapter.

2
Marriage

First you have to be married.

This isn't as silly as it may sound. A "valid and subsisting marriage" carries with it legal rights and obligations that obviously don't exist between unmarried partners.

A valid and subsisting marriage depends on having the capacity to marry and usually (but not always) observing the formal requirements for solemnization of marriage according to the laws of the province in which the marriage is performed, such as obtaining a licence or publishing banns (the announcement within a church of intention to wed), and going through some form of ceremony.

Age of Consent

You have to be old enough to get married. The laws of each province establish an "age of consent", meaning that persons below this age are supposed to obtain permission to marry from one of their parents. By province, the age of consent is: Nova Scotia and

Prince Edward Island, sixteen; Alberta, Manitoba, New Brunswick, Ontario and Quebec, eighteen; British Columbia, Newfoundland and Saskatchewan, nineteen.

If nobody has status to give consent, the licence may be issued without it. Nobody under age fourteen has capacity to marry unless to prevent illegitimacy of an expected child. Where parental consent is unreasonably or arbitrarily withheld, or if it isn't clear who should be giving consent, an application may be made to a judge for an order dispensing with consent.

Mental Capacity to Marry

You must have the mental capacity to understand the nature of the marriage contract, and the duties and responsibilities that it creates. A person who is demonstrably insane at the time of the solemnization has not formed a valid marriage.

Consent of the Parties

You must truly consent to the marriage as a free agent. This means that there must be no duress or force inducing the marriage, nor any misunderstanding as to the effect of the marriage ceremony.

Consanguinity

Your spouse must not be too closely related to you.

4

Each province has established "prohibited degrees of consanguinity", blood relationships which prevent valid marriage. You already know that brother and sister can't marry, but did you know, for example, that a man can't marry his ex-wife's aunt? Information about the prohibited degrees of consanguinity is available wherever marriage licences are issued.

Prior Marriages

You musn't already be married to someone else. Lots of people are already married in a strict legal sense. So if you were previously married and your spouse is still alive, that prior marriage must have been effectively dissolved by divorce or annulment (or death) before you can marry again.*

This is no problem if, say, the prior marriage was solemnized in Saskatchewan, the spouses always lived there together, and later got divorced there. But the situation can become greatly complicated where the prior marriage (or marriages) were solemnized in one place and dissolved in another. Suppose for instance that the wife was first married in California, moved with her husband to New York, got a Mexi-

---

*There is another way. If your spouse has disappeared and been absent for at least seven years without any information whatever about the spouse in that time, you can apply for a court order permitting remarriage. If the spouse turns up later, your first marriage is still valid and your second marriage is void, and children of it are illegitimate. However, you haven't committed bigamy. The Divorce Act now permits a divorce after three years' disappearance, so applications merely to allow remarriage are infrequent.

can divorce, remarried in Florida and got a second divorce in Massachusetts after several years of separation. Now she wants to marry again in Ontario. Before she can marry again she'll have to satisfy the authorities that the divorces validly dissolved the prior marriages. In this example, they probably did, but that's not always the case. In order to apply for a marriage licence, the lady in question must obtain an opinion from a lawyer that she's properly divorced, and file an affidavit — a sworn statement — that says, in effect, that she and her proposed new husband accept sole responsibility in the event that she isn't properly divorced. If it's absolutely necessary to clarify the effect of previous divorces, an interested party can apply to court for a declaratory judgment stating that this is so, but that may be an expensive and lengthy process.

Sometimes people can't be bothered straightening these matters out, so they say nothing about prior marriage when applying for a licence. This runs the risk of committing bigamy, which is still prosecuted as a very serious offence.

Annulment

In the chapter on annulment we'll consider the distinction between marriage that is void *ab initio* (from the beginning) because of lack of capacity, and a marriage that is merely voidable. The latter arises most frequently in a situation where the parties had the capacity to marry but the marriage couldn't be consummated by at least the minimal sexual relationship (penetration of the vagina and emission of semen) that the law requires in order to complete and validate the marriage.

An Exception to the Rule

At the beginning of this chapter, it was stated that parties usually have to observe the formal requirements of a licence or banns and the prescribed ceremony, but there are exceptions. A valid marriage may exist where the parties had the capacity to marry, obtained no licence nor published banns, but went through some form of ceremony followed by cohabitation and particularly by birth of children. This takes care of situations where because of age parental consent was required but not obtained. In one case, it also validated a marriage where the husband specifically and intentionally avoided the formal requirements of solemnization, in the hope that his wife would not gain rights to any of his property.

Rights and Obligations of Marriage

Although a full survey of the legal effects of marriage is beyond the scope of this book, some should be noted.

A valid and subsisting marriage confers the right, and perhaps the duty, to cohabit — to live together as husband and wife—although, as we'll see, this may be ended by various types of misconduct and by agreement.

While the right to cohabit exists, the wife is generally entitled to be financially supported by the husband, but not the other way around.

One aspect of cohabitation as husband and wife is the sexual relationship that the law expects will exist between a married couple. A persistent and unjustified refusal of sexual relations by one spouse may constitute "constructive desertion", relieving the other of the obligation to cohabit.

If the wife is in desertion, the husband is entitled to leave, and he will not be liable to pay alimony to her. If the husband deserts, she is entitled to leave, and the husband will have to pay her alimony.

The right to cohabitation may also be ended by adultery, cruelty, or the more common form of desertion characterized by moving out and failing to provide the necessaries of life. Adultery, cruelty and desertion are the grounds on which a wife can sue her husband for alimony, or take him to Family Court for a support order. Adultery and cruelty are also grounds for divorce, but desertion as such is not.

Husbands and wives have rights to share in the estate after the death of the other, especially if the deceased left no will. Sometimes a spouse and dependent children can get a court order awarding them a share of an estate even though the will of the deceased cut them out.

Lastly, in words from "Porgy and Bess", "You can't divorce people what ain't even married." More often than you might think, a divorce petition fails because the petitioner can't prove that he or she is *validly* married, as in a case where there is a serious question about the validity of a prior divorce decree. Indeed, "That's a complication!"

3
Separation

The Separation Agreement

Many people first approach a lawyer because they
want a "legal separation".

What they usually mean is a separation agreement.
This is a written contract between husband and wife,
much like any other contract, in which they agree to
live apart from each other, and leave each other
alone. Such an agreement is a voluntary act of the
parties. Nobody can be forced to sign a separation
agreement or have one imposed on him by a court or
any other authority.

The amount which should be paid under an agreement must necessarily be determined by negotiation,
but in considering the amount and advising the client,
a lawyer will be thinking what a court might award
in the circumstances of the case. What you pay
must somehow be related to what you might be
ordered to pay. For this reason, and to avoid repetition, the difficult question of amount of maintenance has been included in Chapter 6, dealing with
lawsuits for alimony.

Typically, the opening paragraphs of separation agreements might go something like this:

Neither the husband nor any person on his behalf will at any future time directly or indirectly molest, annoy, disturb or interfere with the wife in her person, business or manner of life, nor at any time require or by any means, either by taking judicial proceedings or otherwise, endeavour to compel the resumption of cohabitation between the husband and wife or to enforce any restitution of conjugal rights and will not for that purpose use any force or restraint to the person of the wife or sue or cause to be sued any person or persons for receiving, protecting or entertaining her. Nothing in this indenture contained shall prevent the bringing in the future of any action for divorce by either of the husband or wife against the other, but if any such action should be brought by the wife against the husband, the provisions of this indenture may be pleaded as an answer to any claim asserted in such action for alimony, interim alimony or maintenance for herself and shall constitute a full and complete defence thereto. The wife shall be free from the control and authority of her husband as if she were unmarried and, subject to the provisions hereinafter contained respecting the residence of the children, may reside at such place as she shall think fit.

Neither the wife nor any person on her behalf will at any future time directly or indirectly molest, annoy, disturb or interfere with the husband in his person, business, or manner of life, nor at any time require or by any means, either by taking judicial proceedings or otherwise, endeavour to compel the resumption of the cohabitation between the husband and wife or to enforce any restitution of conjugal relations.

Just by the way, the language of these paragraphs, which looks like so much hateful legalese to the layman, has been tested hundreds of times in court. That's why lawyers love it. They know what it means, and they know that they can expect a predictable interpretation of this language in a court. When you think of it, that's good for the client, too.

Financial Provisions

Usually a separation agreement will contain financial provisions, perhaps a promise by the husband to pay maintenance for the wife and children for an agreed time, or it may contain a release of any claim for such payments. Payments may run for a fixed term of years, or may be expressed to continue while both parties are alive and so long as the wife does not remarry. It used to be the style to include a *dum casta* clause, so that the wife would be entitled to payments only while she remained chaste, but would lose her right to payments if she had a sexual relationship with another man. In my opinion such a clause has no place in a modern separation agreement, although I am sure that many lawyers would disagree with me. Besides setting up an obviously degrading double standard of conduct, a *dum casta* clause isn't very practical. If the wife takes it seriously, she'll have trouble forming the kind of relationship with another man which could lead to her remarriage. If a husband who enters into a separation agreement really wants to limit his financial obligations, he should encourage his wife towards remarriage, which will end his payments of maintenance.

Now separation agreements more often obligate the husband to pay maintenance for the wife as long as she is not remarried nor living with another man in a husband-and-wife relationship. This is called a *dum sole* clause, meaning literally "while alone".

Some interesting cases have arisen involving separation agreements that, perhaps defectively, lacked both a *dum casta* and a *dum sole* clause. In one, the wife was living in what judges like to call "open adultery", and the husband applied to be relieved of his obligations to pay her under the separation agreement. The effect of the judgment was that he had made a deal, and it was his own fault if he failed adequately to protect himself; payments continued. But in another case, the wife had actually remarried, when the husband applied to stop payments under the separation agreement. The result was different. The court ruled on public-policy grounds that the wife should not be entitled to be maintained by two men, and the ex-husband was excused from further payment.

Maintenance and Custody of Children

Maintenance for children is usually fixed until the children reach an agreed age. Often this age is eighteen, with a provision that the children are entitled to maintenance after age eighteen and until age twenty-one as long as the children are living at home and attending school and have not themselves married.

Custody of the children can be either to one parent, or jointly to both, but the latter arrangement tends to be suitable only when the children are in their early teens, and both parents are involved and concerned with supervision and guidance.

Older children make their own decisions. They just aren't going to be controlled by the agreement of their parents that one or the other have custody. Also, as children grow up, there's a better chance that the relationship between parent and child can survive the separation. If the parents split when the child is, say, three years old, it's likely that if the parent with custody remarries, the new spouse will completely replace the natural parent. But if the child is older, the step-parent may never become a full substitute. And if the children are old enough to truly understand what's happening, they may be extremely upset that one parent has, so to speak, given them up. An agreement for joint custody would be indicated in such a situation.

Access

Visiting rights can be undefined, called "reasonable access", or defined, so that the parent who doesn't have custody is entitled to visit and have the children with him or her at specifically agreed periods. Reasonable access often works well, but it depends on reasonable people. Where the parents are continuingly hostile to each other, access had better be defined. An agreement for reasonable access can contain a clause to permit either parent to apply to court for a definition of access in the event of trouble. But the court probably has power to make an access order on whatever terms may be appropriate, even if the agreement omits this provision.

Other Possible Provisions

The separation agreement may contain clauses covering division of property, payment of debts, responsibility for carrying insurance, release of any interest in each other's estate, and anything else that the situation may demand. The scope of a separation agreement is limited only by the imagination of the parties.

If you need a separation agreement, don't try to do it yourself, even if you and your spouse agree (or think you agree) on all the terms. A separation agreement is a complex, difficult document, as the example above may have demonstrated. You may have to live with your agreement for many years. Only a skilled lawyer has the competence to handle this job, if only by pointing out possible complications that the parties may have overlooked.

Alteration of the Terms

Can the terms of a separation agreement be altered afterwards? The answer, like so many answers to legal problems, is that it depends . . . .

Yes, if the agreement contains clauses which permit variation, as many do. Such provisions may require the husband to pay an additional percentage of his income if it rises above an agreed level, and may allow him to reduce payments if it falls below that level. Fluctuation of payments, up or down, may be tied to the official cost-of-living index. The agreement may contain broad and general variation provisions, recognizing the potential need to make other arrangements for the benefit of the parties and their children as circumstances change. A modern tendency is to include a clause stating that, in the event of a material change, either party has the right to apply to the other to renegotiate; if the parties can't agree on a variation, then either has the right to submit the problem to an arbitrator, who will hear the submissions of the parties, and make a decision. The parties agree to be bound by the arbitration, but usually the separation agreement will provide that either has a right of appeal from the award of the arbitrator to a regular court.

Arbitration clauses are more popular with wives, who are generally on the receiving end of separation agreements and concerned to cover contingencies. Husbands usually want their obligations fixed once and for all. Arbitration opens up the possibility of changing the terms of the agreement, and not too many husbands are sufficiently filled with goodwill at the time of a marital split to want this flexibility.

Yes, a separation agreement may be altered also if a court needs to make an order contrary to the terms of the agreement for the benefit of the children. The parties can agree on custody, access and maintenance, but no court is bound by this if, on hearing evidence, the judge concludes that the welfare of the children demands some other arrangement.

The terms of the agreement may also be changed within the context of a petition for divorce. Under the Divorce Act, the court which hears the petition has power to make orders for "corollary relief" — support payments, custody of children and visiting rights — and in doing so is clearly not bound by the terms of a separation agreement. However, the court will not lightly disregard the provisions of a separation agreement, which, after all, expressed the wishes of the parties when it was signed. Thus there have been very few decisions in divorce cases where an agreement was overridden by the presiding judge.

Why Is a Separation Agreement a Good Idea?

There seems to be a common misconception that husband and wife must have a separation agreement before they can embark on a divorce. This is absolutely false; but it's a good idea to work out a separation agreement if divorce is contemplated. Parties who have an agreement usually have nothing left to fight about when the divorce petition is launched, so that the divorce can proceed as an undefended case, with the separation agreement approved by the court when the divorce decree is granted. Often, the clauses of the separation agreement which deal with corollary relief can be incorporated right into the divorce decree. It's quicker and far less expensive to settle corollary relief by negotiation and resulting separation agreement than it is to fight it out in court. And very importantly, a separation agreement can cover areas beyond the jurisdiction of a court granting alimony or corollary relief, such as insurance, providing a car, club memberships, use of charge accounts and anything else that the needs and imaginations of the parties may suggest.

But apart from the above situations, which I grant you cover a lot of ground, a separation agreement can no more be varied by a court than can any other contract in writing, and any lawyer will tell you that judges are extremely reluctant to do that.

Enforcement

A separation agreement can be enforced just like any other contract. If payments are in default, you can sue on the contract for a judgment entitling you to collect by seizure of assets, including wages. If for example, the husband harasses the wife despite his promise to leave her alone, the wife can apply for an injunction restraining the husband from continuing his harassment; if he persists he runs the risk of a citation for contempt of court and a possible jail term. A wife who violates the terms of a separation agreement may disentitle herself to payment of maintenance or other benefits under the agreement.

While the parties are continuing to live up to the terms of the agreement, a separation agreement is a complete defence to any claim contrary to the terms of the agreement, subject to the possibility of variation imposed by a court as noted above. For example, a wife who goes to Family Court claiming maintenance because she was deserted will not succeed if she has signed a separation agreement, as long as the agreement has been honoured: a wife who has agreed to live apart from her husband can hardly be deserted.

But if the agreement has been breached, it is usually open to either party to make any claim that would have been available if there had never been an agreement at all.

Duration of The Terms

The terms of a separation agreement generally are expressed to continue after the parties are divorced, so that the divorce as such will not end, say, the husband's obligation to pay maintenance, provide insurance etc. Also, if the corollary relief provisions of the agreement are included in the divorce decree, the other terms survive in full force.

Even if it doesn't say so specifically, a separation agreement ends in all its terms if the parties effect a genuine reconciliation. If they break up after that, the agreement is not revived. Go back to Square One and start again. So as to avoid any wrangling over the genuineness of a reconciliation, many separation agreements provide that if the parties at any time resume cohabitation for a given period, say, sixty days, the agreement will be void.

Decree of Judicial Separation

In provinces other than Ontario, it's possible to sue

for a decree of judicial separation. This is a court order declaring that the parties no longer need live together as husband and wife, and fixing terms of maintenance, custody and access. This is often confused with a separation agreement, and is what some people mean when they speak of a "legal separation". It's a useful remedy when the right to cohabitation has ended because of a marital offence, such as adultery, cruelty or desertion (discussed in the chapter on alimony), and the offending party refuses to enter into a separation agreement. Of course, a decree of judicial separation does not dissolve the marriage.

A Suggestion

If the husband wants out, especially where there's another woman waiting for him, the best separation agreement is likely to be the quickest separation agreement. A husband who feels guilty about leaving his family often wants to ease his conscience by paying the maximum maintenance, and agreeing to all sorts of fringe benefits. Wait a few weeks and he'll realize that he loathes his wife and can do without his children. Guilt turns to relief, and he's tougher about money.

4
Family Court

What Is Family Court?

Each province has some kind of Family Court,
which provides the legal machinery to enable wives
to get money from erring husbands relatively quickly
and cheaply.

In every case the procedure is to lay an information (the sworn statement used to start criminal
proceedings), or else to file a form of complaint
whereupon a judge will issue the summons. The
husband is served personally with the summons, or
it's mailed to him or served at his residence or
business, just as if he were summonsed to appear to
a criminal charge. In fact, this is one of the frequent
complaints about Family Courts: husbands say that
they don't mind so much appearing in court, but they
hate it when a uniformed police officer serves them
with a summons at work.

In any event, when the case comes before the
judge or magistrate or justice of the peace, the wife
must also appear and tell her story. She doesn't
really need a lawyer in Family Court, and in fact,

the Family Court is designed (theoretically) for a kind of rough justice, which often seems to conflict with a lawyer's attitude to the niceties of evidence and formal court procedure.

Remember that in Family Court, the wife is always the complainant against the husband. She needs money for herself and/or the children. The judge (or whoever) is likely to look on the case as a social problem as much as or more than a legal problem. And by the way, this is one place where you *don't* always have to be married. Certainly it makes no difference in Family Court if the question at stake is support for the children, and the parents never "made it legal". One province, Nova Scotia, for purposes of Family Court jurisdiction, defines a wife to include a woman who has lived with a man for not less than five years, so that she can get maintenance in Family Court.

Basis of Family Court Order

In every province (except Quebec), the wife must show that she has been deserted, a term that is variously defined. Each province includes as one element of desertion a failure, neglect or refusal to provide the necessaries of life; in Nova Scotia the definition stops right there. Each other province extends the definition to include cruelty, and, except for New Brunswick, adultery as well. In B.C., Manitoba, Newfoundland and P.E.I., the definition is extended to include excessive drinking.

Maintenance

Typically, the Family Courts used to have some sort of monetary limit on the amount they could order the husband to pay, but except in New Brunswick and P.E.I. these limits have been repealed. The one wrinkle is that in B.C., Newfoundland and P.E.I., there is a rider that in no event can the Family Court order more than one-half of the amount necessary for the maintenance of the children if the wife has means of her own.

Child Custody

The Family Courts also have some jurisdiction over child custody, as noted later in the chapter on custody. But the power to award custody is always incidental to ordering maintenance for children who have been deserted. Thus the father can not get custody in Family Court, no matter what theoretical power the judge or magistrate may appear to have under the provincial statute.

Family Court versus "Superior Court"

Problems often arise in a conflict of jurisdictions between, say, the Family Court and the superior court of a province. Both can make orders for support of wives and children, and grant custody and access.

Suppose, for example, that the wife got an order for custody and maintenance of the children in

Family Court, and now her husband proceeds with a divorce petition, where he doesn't make any claim for custody. What happens to the outstanding Family Court order? The answer is that a Family Court order for the maintenance of children is not terminated by dissolution of the marriage. The order can be (and often is) incorporated into the divorce decree on the same terms, and enforced as if it were an order for "corollary relief". Or it may not be included in the decree, and it can still be enforced through the Family Court. There is also a recent ruling that if the divorce decree says nothing at all about maintenance for the children, the Family Court still has jurisdiction to order support for them.

Effect of Divorce on Family Court Order

Dissolution of the marriage terminates a Family Court order for maintenance of the wife. When she's no longer married, she no longer has the right of support. The wife can, and should, protect herself by getting an order for maintenance in the divorce proceedings, to replace a Family Court order previously obtained. But if she fails to do so, her right to support is forever lost, since the divorce court has power to make a maintenance order only upon granting the decree. The wife can't come along later and get maintenance for herself on the basis that she forgot, or that now she only wants the decree varied to assist her. In one very tough judgment it was ruled that the wife could not obtain such relief even where her lawyers were mistaken about the effect of the divorce decree on an outstanding Family Court order for maintenance. They apparently thought that the maintenance order would continue in spite of the divorce. It doesn't.

Effect of Separation Agreement on Family Court Order

The Supreme Court of Canada has decided that where there is a valid and subsisting separation agreement, the wife cannot be deserted within the definition used in Family Court. That makes sense. If the parties have agreed to live apart, the wife should not later have the option of invoking the aid of the Family Court to try for a better deal. In one extreme application of this rule, a dissatisfied wife had left her husband, taking the six children of the marriage with her. The husband, who had not been guilty of adultery, cruelty or desertion, stayed in the home, and desperately wanted his family to return. The wife consulted lawyers of her own choosing, on whose advice she signed a separation agreement absolving the husband from any responsibility to pay maintenance for herself or the children. Then she went to Family Court claiming that the husband had deserted the children in the sense that he was refusing to provide for them. The husband said, firstly, just send the kids home and I'll be glad to look after them; secondly, there's a separation agreement, so I haven't deserted them. The judge reluctantly agreed, dismissing the wife's claim. But the Court of Appeal ruled that a father can't contract out of his obligations to his children, and ordered him to pay maintenance.

Of course, if there's a separation agreement, but the husband hasn't complied with its terms, he loses that defence and the court can deal with the case as if there were no separation agreement at all.

Other Complications

Conflicts can arise in other ways. In one reported case, the wife claimed for maintenance in a divorce petition, but while the divorce hearing was pending, she went to Family Court for a maintenance order. The ruling was that in this situation the Family Court had no power to help her. On the other hand, it has been decided that the Family Court has the power to rule on the custody of and access to children while the same issues are pending in a divorce petition.

If the wife starts an action for alimony, it amounts to abandonment of her rights under a Family Court order, so that if her alimony claim fails, she can't fall back on the previous award. But the fact that she has previously gone to Family Court, successfully or not, isn't a defence available to the husband if she later decides to sue for alimony.

The Family Court may find that the husband has been guilty of adultery as an element of "desertion", but this isn't evidence of adultery that can later be used as the basis for a divorce. Most provinces cover this by specific language, such as contained in the Ontario statute: "A finding by the judge that adultery has been proved is not evidence of the adultery in any other proceedings."

Enforcement

If the husband doesn't obey a support order, the Family Court has its own easily accessible enforcement procedures. He can be brought before the court to explain his default, put on terms as to payment, ordered to pay arrears by a certain date. If default continues, he can be put in jail, not for his debt (we don't have debtors' prisons), but for his disobedience of a court order.

In most provinces this enforcement machinery is also available for alimony orders and maintenance orders made in divorce cases, including interim orders. All the wife need do is file a copy of the order with the Family Court, so that in the event of default she can take advantage of its inexpensive and relatively speedy procedures to help her collect the money.

Following is a comparative table of information about Family Courts in the ten provinces.

FAMILY COURTS IN CANADA

	Statute	Court	Grounds	Proceed by	Monetary Limit
ALTA.	Domestic Relations Act	Magistrate's Court	Desertion: cruelty or failure to provide	Summons	None
B.C.	Wives' and Children's Maintenance Act	Family and Children's Court	Desertion: assaults, cruelty, failure to provide, drunkenness or adultery	Summons	None*
MAN.	Wives' and Children's Maintenance Act	County Court	Assault, desertion, cruelty, habitual drunkenness or failure to provide	Summons	None
N.B.	Deserted Wives' and Children's Maintenance Act	Magistrate's, Juvenile or County Court	Desertion: cruelty or failure to provide	Summons	$30 per week for wife; $10 per week each child

NFLD.	Maintenance Act	Family or Magistrate's Court, or two J.P.'s	Desertion: assaults, cruelty, failure to provide, drunkenness or adultery	Summons	None*
N.S.	Wives' and Children's Maintenance Act	Magistrate's Court	Desertion: failure to provide	Summons	None
ONT.	Deserted Wives' and Children's Maintenance Act	Provincial Court (Family Division)	Desertion: cruelty, failure to provide or adultery	Summons	None
P.E.I.	Children's Act	County Court	Desertion: assaults, cruelty, failure to provide, drunkenness or adultery	Complaint: judge issues summons	$40. per week*
QUE.	Civil Code, Section 175	Superior Court	Failure to provide (insufficient allowance)	Motion to Court	None
SASK.	Deserted Wives' and Children's Maintenance Act	District or Magistrate's Court	Desertion: failure to provide, cruelty or adultery	Complaint: judge issues summons	None

*If wife has means, not to exceed half of amount necessary for maintenance of children

5

Custody and Maintenance of Children

Custody proceedings can be undertaken by either parent independently of any other claim, or linked with some other type of relief, where one parent wants to have sole care and control of the children.

The point is *sole* control. Unless and until a court order is made granting custody to one parent, the parents stand in absolute equality in their right to custody of the children. The words of the Ontario Infant's Act make this plain: "Unless otherwise ordered by a court . . . the father and mother of an infant are joint guardians and are equally entitled to the custody, control and education of the infant." Each province has similar legislation.

This may be hard to believe in view of the prevalent myth that the mother *always* gets custody of the children. It just isn't so, if we're talking about what happens in court, except Family Court. In law, neither party has an inside track, even if the children are very young.

Of course, in a practical sense, the mother certainly does get custody more often than the father; but that's because in so many cases where the parents have split up, there's no argument about custody, and the matter isn't contested in court: In a situation where the father is working and the mother is not, where the children are very young, where the father doesn't want custody, where the father wants custody but doesn't feel competent to look after the children — the mother will usually get custody by agreement or default.

But once the parties are in front of a judge, the basic principle governing the award of custody is that *the welfare of the children is the paramount consideration.* Not the convenience of the parties. Not even the agreement of the parties. The welfare of the children overrides any other factor.

How to Apply for Custody

There are five ways to get an application for custody before a court in Ontario. These procedures are roughly similar in each province of Canada.

1. Family Court

As described in the previous chapter, the mother may make an application for child custody to the Provincial Court (Family Division), usually known as the Family Court, incidental to a claim for maintenance (support) of the child under a statute called The Deserted Wives' and Children's Maintenance Act.

The mother goes to the office of the Family Court and swears an "information", a statement that the father is in breach of the Deserted Wives' and Children's Maintenance Act; then a police officer

31

serves the father with a summons to appear in court, in just the same way as if the father were charged with a criminal offence.

The operative section of the Act states that if the father has wilfully refused or neglected to maintain the child and has deserted the child, the court may order the father to pay for the support of the child such sum at such intervals as the judge considers proper, having regard to the means of the father and to any means the child may have for his own support. A child is deserted by his father when the child is under the age of sixteen, or is sixteen or seventeen years old and in full-time attendance at an educational institution; and the father has, without adequate cause, refused or neglected to supply the child with food or other necessaries when able to do so.

In awarding maintenance the judge may make an order for custody of and access to the child for any person, or for either parent, having regard to the welfare of the child and to the conduct of the parent or person and to the wishes of the parents. And the judge may at any time alter, vary or discharge any such order.

Although this Act empowers the judge to award custody to *any* person, the father can never get custody in Family Court, since the jurisdiction of that court depends on a finding that the father deserted the child, and then custody can only be granted incidental to an order for maintenance. Of course, when appropriate or necessary, custody might be awarded to someone other than the mother.

In the Family Court, the existence of a separation agreement will invariably defeat a claim that the child has been deserted, as long as the terms of the agreement are being met. However, if the father is in breach of the separation agreement (say, as to payment of support for the child), the agreement is no defence, and he can be found to have deserted the child.

2. Infant's Act

An application for child custody can be made by either parent under the Infant's Act, either to a judge of the Supreme Court, or to a judge of the Surrogate Court of the county in which the infant is living at the time the proceedings are commenced.

This procedure is started by a notice of motion, a document giving to the other parent at least seven days' notice of the application. The motion is generally supported by the affidavit of the applicant setting out the facts on which the applicant relies in his or her claim for custody. The notice of motion and affidavit are served by delivery of copies of these documents to the other party, called the respondent, and then the applicant files the documents at the court office for the use of the judge. The respondent may also serve and file an affidavit setting out facts in opposition to the applicant's claim for custody, and perhaps asking that custody be granted to the respondent. Both parties may then be cross-examined on the contents of their affidavits at the office of a court reporter, their attendance being arranged by appointment agreed to by the opposing lawyers, or compelled by subpoena. Transcripts of the examinations will be filed for the use of the judge hearing the application.

The court has power to make such order as it sees fit regarding the custody of the infant and the right of access to the child of either parent, "having regard to the welfare of the infant, and to the conduct of the parents and to the wishes as well of the mother as of the father, and may alter, vary or discharge the order on the application of either parent. . . ."

By the time conflicting affidavits and transcripts of cross-examinations have been filed, the court will be faced with a hopelessly contradictory and controversial mass of material. In Supreme Court, the judge hearing the application will frequently rule that he cannot choose between the competing claims on the basis of that material, so he will direct a trial on the issue — saying, in effect, go have a real court case; call all the witnesses you wish to testify. He will designate one of the parties to be plaintiff and the other defendant, and will give directions for the procedure to be followed to bring the case on for hearing in due course.

In Surrogate Court the procedure is a little different. The judge, instead of directing a trial, will often appoint a date when he will hear witnesses, and decide the matter. This is a speedier process than an application in Supreme Court if a trial is directed, and much more convenient if the parties are living in a small town where a Surrogate Court judge is available, but a Supreme Court judge is not.

In Ontario and British Columbia, the judge may instruct the Official Guardian to investigate and deliver a report to assist and advise the court. This means the parents will be visited and interviewed by a social worker, who will deliver a report in prescribed form describing the proposal of each parent for custody and maintenance of the children, and the character of the parents and children themselves.

The court also has a general power to call for expert assistance. Sometimes this is used to obtain a psychiatric assessment of the children and parents, in a report prepared by an independent psychiatrist appointed by the court or agreed to by both parties.

3. Alimony Action

A claim for custody can be made by the mother as plaintiff in an alimony action, and incidental to her claim for alimony. The father might counter-claim for custody. For procedure, see Chapter 6, "Alimony".

4. Divorce Petition

A claim for custody can be made by either parent as corollary relief in a divorce petition or counter-petition. The Divorce Act says that corollary relief can be awarded only upon the granting of a divorce decree; but in a few cases the court has dismissed the divorce petition, and yet granted custody and maintenance for the children anyway, exercising its general jurisdiction over infants, or utilizing the statutory powers contained in equivalents of the Infant's Act. For procedure, see Chapter 7, "Divorce".

5. General Jurisdiction

An application for custody can be made by anyone, whether a parent or not, invoking the general jurisdiction of the Supreme Court to make orders for the welfare of infants. This application is made without reference to any statute, but rather because of a power that the Supreme Court acquired when given the same jurisdiction as the courts of England had.

The procedure starts by issuing a writ of summons in the Supreme Court claiming custody, and then following the formal steps to bring the suit on for hearing, just like any other lawsuit. A complete survey of this procedure would amount to a law-school course, and is too technical and various for the scope of this book.

This method is used especially when a person who is not a parent of the child wants to be granted custody. It usually involves competing claims by, say, an aunt who raised the child, and the natural mother of the child.

Note that all the procedures but this one can only be commenced by a parent of the child, although in the context of any of them the court can award custody to anybody. It sometimes happens just that way. The judge may, on an application for custody, be unimpressed by the competing claims of the parents and their ability to do right by the children, so that he grants custody to the grandparents who have been looking after the children all along.

The Guiding Principle in Custody Cases

If the welfare of the children is the paramount consideration governing an award of custody, then the practical statement of that principle must be: "He who has custody, gets custody."

You won't find that in the law books, but it's true. You *will* find in the law books an expression of that principle where an award of interim custody is concerned. An application for interim custody arises in connection with a claim for interim alimony, or with an application for interim corollary relief in a divorce petition, or at any time when the matter of custody can't be dealt with right away, but must be deferred for some reason. That's where a lot of custody fights are won and lost, on the application for interim custody. Here's why.

He who has custody, gets custody: the leading case on interim custody says that, in the absence of very cogent evidence to the contrary, the children should stay where they are pending a final disposition of the custody claim.

Suppose, for example, that the mother leaves the father, taking the children with her. She starts a claim for custody under one of the procedures already outlined, for example under the Infant's Act in Supreme Court, or the equivalent statute in her home province. She arranges some sort of home for the children; maybe it's not materially as good as the one they had before the parents split, but the children are decently fed, clothed, and aren't being neglected. Let's say her motion for custody is opposed by the father, and turned into a directed trial of a custody issue. The mother has the established rule governing award of interim custody going for her, so the judge rules that the mother should have interim custody of the children pending trial. Under *ideal* conditions it will take several months for this case to be heard and the final disposition of custody to be made, and it may take a lot longer. During this time, the mother has stabilized the situation for the children. They've adjusted. They're at a new school, with new friends. The mother has a job. Day-care arrangements appear satisfactory. The father has been paying interim maintenance for the children and seeing them regularly.

Well, if you were the trial judge, what would you do? Why uproot the children now, after they've been through so much? Agreed, the mother isn't perfect: maybe the father could buy more for the children. But the kids are doing all right. Better the devil you know than the devil you don't know. Result: custody to the mother with reasonable access to the father; maintenance of so much a week for the children payable by the father.

The mother had custody, and she got custody. In effect, this case was over when she was granted interim custody.

Kidnapping Is No Solution

If you think the way to solve the problem is to "kidnap" the children, you're absolutely wrong. The courts have consistently ruled against this kind of attempt at self-help. No judge wants to see the children shuffled from one hiding place to another because of the competing claims of the parents.

Attempts at self-help sometimes reach extremes. Believing that the courts of a given province will not rule on the custody of a child unless the child is resident in that province, a parent will sometimes snatch the child and flee to another province (or country), in the hope that custody proceedings in the home province will be defeated. It's very unlikely to work. The court of the home province will usually rule that the child is ordinarily resident in that province, and take jurisdiction to make a custody order.

In one Ontario case, while the mother's claim for interim custody was pending, the father called his lawyer from the airport on a Saturday morning, saying that he had the child, and was just getting on a plane for Saskatchewan. It didn't help him. The court subsequently ruled that he couldn't defeat the court's power to make a custody order by running away, and granted custody to the mother.

In another recent decision, the ordinary residence of the children was in Ontario. The father had grabbed the children and taken them to northern British Columbia, where he left them in the care of the woman with whom he was living. The wife brought a claim for custody in Ontario. The judge ruled that since the children were ordinarily resident in Ontario, he had jurisdiction, and he awarded the mother custody of the children.

If an applicant gets a custody order, but the children are not physically resident in the province where the order was granted, the applicant still has the problem of enforcing the order in another place. Generally, the courts of that other place will give "grave consideration" to the custody order. But they are not bound by it, unless the award of custody derives from the corollary-relief provisions of the Divorce Act, because an order made under the Divorce Act has legal effect throughout Canada.

A few months ago a case arose where the parents had been living together in Denmark with their child. They split up, and the mother got an order granting her custody of the child. The father snatched the child and fled to Ontario. The lawyer for the mother in Ontario applied for custody there, relying heavily on the previous order made in Denmark, the ordinary residence of the child. Afraid that the husband might flee again, he cleverly got an interim order that the child be placed in temporary custody of the Danish consul in Toronto until the matter was decided. The mother's application was decided summarily in her favour, with no trial directed, and an appeal by the father failed.

A distinction should be made between these "kidnap" cases, and a situation where a previous custody order has been largely disregarded by the parents by agreement, so that the court must rule on the effect of a custody order made in another jurisdiction, but now perhaps obsolete because of changed circumstances. The court will certainly give consideration to that order, but will in no way be bound by it.

Review of Custody Orders

No custody order is ever final. Any custody order is open to review, simply because the welfare of the children may from time to time demand that another order be made. Parents can certainly agree on custody, as they often do in separation agreements, but no such agreement is binding on a court.

Guiding Sub-Principles

There are other sub-principles which guide the court in awarding custody:

— When other things between the parents are equal, it is presumed that children of "tender years" need the care of the mother more than the father. This applies up to the age of seven, approximately. Beyond this age, custody of sons might more likely be given to the father, and custody of daughters to the mother, if there is no other basis for making a choice.

— The court will lean away from separating siblings.

— The court will consider the wishes of older children as to which parent should have custody. Probably a judge would listen to a child of ten, certainly to a teen-age child. As a practical matter, custody fights rarely occur over older children anyway. What are you going to do if a fourteen-year-old simply doesn't want to live with you? That's why the wishes of an older child might as well be considered, because an order made contrary to his wishes is likely to be ignored by the child himself, or else enforced by compulsion creating increased misery. The real knock-down, drag-out custody fights take place over younger children for just this reason: custody of a six-year-old can be enforced no matter what the child wants.

— Natural parents of a child can only lose custody by abandoning the child, or so misconducting themselves that, in the opinion of the court, it would be improper for the child to remain with them. This will depend entirely on the facts of the individual case.

Lawyers have often observed that there's no more bitter and dirty type of case than a hard-fought custody trial. Partly that's because of the incalculably

41

high stakes. But partly it results from the fact that one way to bolster your case is to make the other parent look as destructive and incompetent as possible. For this purpose, nearly anything in the conduct of the parents is relevant to the welfare of the children, so no evidentiary holds are barred. Anything goes, and the parents compete in a mud-slinging match.

Custody by Agreement

Fortunately, relatively few custody disputes get to trial. Most are settled by agreement, because having regard to the principles which motivate the court, the result is highly predictable. If, for example, the mother has had interim custody of the children for a year while the trial was pending, the father has little hope of winning permanent custody at trial. Why waste the time, money and emotional energy that get used up in a trial?

Unless the father is so stubborn or self-righteous that he doesn't care what it costs him (not only financially but psychologically), he'd be better off to forget about custody, and concentrate on working out a sensible access arrangement. The mother may be willing to agree on far more generous access than a court would award, in order to avoid the pain and expense of a trial. Also, if they settle, both parents can probably live with the deal, since it is of their own making; and their future relationship with each other and the children isn't poisoned by the traumatic memory of the trial.

The Hollow Threat

There is a common belief that a mother who commits adultery deprives herself of custody of the children. I'd like a nickel for every woman who has been terrified by a threat from her husband that he'll take the children away and she'll never see them again because she has been unfaithful. Even where the husband and wife have been separated for years, this threat still arises. It simply isn't true. A mother who commits adultery is not disentitled to custody on that ground, and will be granted custody when to do so is in the best interests of the child. This applies even if the mother is living with another man. The welfare of the child governs. The courts no longer assume that an unfaithful wife is an unfit mother.

Visiting Rights (Access)

Access includes the right to visit the child and take the child away from the home under certain conditions. It's almost always granted. About the only way to bar a parent from access is to convince the court that a positive physical, emotional, moral or spiritual harm will result if that parent has access to the child. Obviously, that's hard to do. Often a custody case ends in an atmosphere of hostility and bitterness. If the mother is granted custody, she's likely to be terribly upset that the father has been granted access. But in many cases, whether for good or bad, the parent who loses custody just drifts off the scene after a few months, and never or seldom exercises the access to which he is entitled.

Access can be undefined, so-called "reasonable access", meaning, in effect, let the parents work it out themselves. As stated earlier, reasonable access depends on reasonable people. If the parents are fairly amiable to each other, the flexibility of reasonable access works just fine, and is to be preferred.

Naturally, in many cases the parents hate each other, and try to interfere with access so as to be as punitive as possible. Then "defined access" is indicated, the kind of order that specifies the precise days and times that the non-custodial parent may have the child. Sometimes access starts as reasonable, but that doesn't work out, the parties have to go back to court to have access defined. Like a custody order, an access order is always open to review.

Access has a practical base similar to custody. A six-year-old will go with the visiting parent whenever access is exercised, but a twelve-year-old often has his own time organized in a way that may not suit an access order. Well, what can you do? There's no effective way to compel an older child to submit to a visiting arrangement if he doesn't want to do it.

A real fight may develop if custody has been settled by a separation agreement containing a provision that, say, neither parent will remove the children from the province for more than three weeks without first obtaining the written consent of the other. Let's suppose the mother has custody under such an agreement, signed when all the parties were living in New Brunswick. Now she wants to move with the children to Alberta. The father who has a right of access under the agreement may try to restrain her from moving by applying for an injunction, but he's rather unlikely to succeed.

The parent who has custody is usually entitled to move with the children away from the place where custody was granted or agreed to, although it means that the other parent will find it inconvenient or impossible to exercise access. The right of access cannot prevail over the right of custody.

Custody of Illegitimate Children

Suppose the child is illegitimate? There's no question that the mother has the prime right to custody of an illegitimate child. Some would have said that the father has no right of custody at all, but several decisions in the last year or so make it perfectly clear that the father of an illegitimate child has the right to apply for custody of, or access to, the child. In Ontario, the Infant's Act permits such an application to be made by the mother *or* the father — it doesn't say anything about the parents being married — and all provinces have similar legislation.

The father of an illegitimate child definitely doesn't start from the same position of equality as he would if the parents were married; he has an uphill fight to convince a court that he should be granted access, much less custody, because of the prime right of the mother.

Child Support (Maintenance)

Maintenance is the term applied to the financial support that a parent is obligated to give a child. The basic statutory provision in Ontario is found in the Children's Maintenance Act, and the legislation is similar in other provinces. It states that every parent shall maintain and educate his child up to age sixteen in accordance with his ability to do so, and the child's ability to maintain himself. Failure to do so constitutes an offence for which the guilty parent can be imprisoned for up to three months.

Also, under the Criminal Code, everyone is under a duty as a parent, foster parent, guardian or head of a family to provide necessaries of life for a child under the age of sixteen, with penalties ranging up to imprisonment for two years for failure to do so.

An order directing payment of maintenance can be made in several ways:

— In Family Court, under the terms of the Deserted Wives' and Children's Maintenance Act, as previously noted, a father who deserts a child can be ordered to pay maintenance for him to age sixteen, or to age eighteen if the child is in full-time attendance at an educational institution.

— In Supreme Court or Surrogate Court, under the Infant's Act, "the court may . . . make an order for the maintenance of the infant by payment by the father . . . of such sum from time to time as according to the pecuniary circumstances of the father . . . the court deems reasonable." Note that under the Infant's Act (Ontario) there is no jurisdiction to order the mother to pay maintenance for the children, even if the court grants custody to the father. This obvious loophole should be plugged by legislative amendment in the near future. Under the

Infant's Act, a maintenance order can run to age eighteen.

— In Supreme Court, exercising its inherent power to make orders for the benefit of infants, the court can order either parent to pay maintenance either in the context of an alimony action, or on the application of any interested person. Maintenance can continue to age eighteen.

— In Supreme Court, as corollary relief within the context of a divorce petition, maintenance can be ordered to continue to age sixteen, to age eighteen if the child is dependent, and possibly to any age at all as long as the child remains dependent.

There's no doubt that the Supreme Court can make an order for interim maintenance running until final disposition of any of the proceedings listed above. It's doubtful if a Surrogate Court judge can make an interim order for maintenance under the Infant's Act. And a Family Court judge has no power to make an interim maintenance order under the present legislation.

If the child is illegitimate, the father may be compelled to pay maintenance by a Family Court order made under the Deserted Wives' and Children's Maintenance Act, just as if the parents were married. He may also be summonsed to appear in Family Court in "affiliation" proceedings brought under the Child Welfare Act (Ontario), or equivalent legislation in the home province. This statute enables the mother of an illegitimate child to name the father and compel him to pay maintenance up to age sixteen.

Under a separation agreement, since it is a voluntary contract of the parties, maintenance is often expressed to be paid for much longer than it might be under a court order. Frequently a separation agreement provides that each child will be entitled to maintenance up to age twenty-one (or even longer), provided that the child is living at home and is in full-time attendance at an educational institution, unless the child marries. Such an agreement is enforceable in accordance with its own terms.

Just by the way, an interesting wrinkle is found in a little-used Ontario statute, the Parents' Maintenance Act, which makes children responsible for the maintenance of parents who are dependent because of age, disease or infirmity. The children can be summonsed to court and ordered to pay maintenance for the parents.

Amount of Maintenance

It's impossible to set out a formula for the proper amount of maintenance for children. There is certainly no rule of thumb or percentage of salary that must be allowed. As we've noted before, the correct amount of maintenance will depend on the circumstances of the individual case, and is up to the discretion of the court. Both parents have a legal obligation to maintain the children in accordance with their ability to do so, even in a legal situation where only the father can be *ordered* to pay maintenance. To take an extreme case, if custody is granted to the mother who earns $15,000 a year while the father is out of work, doubtless the father won't be ordered to pay maintenance.

Enforcement of Maintenance Orders

Maintenance orders can be reciprocally enforced from province to province by statutory provisions. It gets a bit cumbersome, though, and in many cases geographical separation of the parents spells the effective end of a maintenance order. Often, if the wife moves away, or even if she stays but obstructs access, the father will complain that he's being asked to pay for the children when he can't visit them. This argument is frequently received with sympathy in court, and the maintenance order is varied or discharged.

Adoption

Where the parents have become divorced and the parent with custody remarries, adoption proceedings may arise. Let's say that the mother has custody after the divorce and remarriage, and her new husband wants to adopt the child. This may be done with the consent of the natural father, and may be done without his consent if he has in effect abandoned the child, for instance by not paying maintenance nor visiting the child. In any event, the natural father must be consulted; and if the adopting parents seek to dispense with his consent, he must be given notice of the application to do so. Once the child is adopted, the natural parent has no further obligation to maintain the child. This may be the selling point in getting the required consent: if you let us adopt, you won't have to pay any more.

The legal effect of adoption varies somewhat from province to province.

Probably the idea in each province is to put the adopted child in *exactly* the same position as a natural and legitimate child of the parents. But the language of statutes and the ingenuity of lawyers being what they are, other interpretations have crept in. The problem usually arises in a fight over money: for example, if in a will the deceased left his estate "to my grandchildren", the question arises whether adopted children of his own children are included. From Ontario west to British Columbia, and in Nova Scotia, the statutes say that for all purposes an adopted child becomes upon adoption the child of the adopting parent, and the adopting parent becomes the parent of the child, as if the child had been born to that parent in lawful wedlock. The other provinces make it less clear. In Quebec the provision is that the adopted child becomes the legitimate child of the adopter and his consort, if the latter joined in the motion for adoption.

Most provinces have procedures for amending the child's original birth certificate after adoption, so that the birth records show the adopting parents as if they were the natural parents, without any reference to the child's pre-adoption name.

A parent who is granted custody may wonder what would happen in the event of his or her death. Would the surviving parent have an absolute right to claim custody of the child? The answer is that the surviving parent would certainly have a considerable claim to custody, but no exclusive right. The court is always empowered to make whatever custody order best serves the welfare of the child. In cases of this sort, it is not at all unusual for another relative or a new spouse to gain custody, as against the claim of the surviving natural parent.

Unfortunately, this problem can't effectively be solved by the terms of a will. Any provision for guardianship or custody contained in a will is merely "precatory", an expression of a wish. It isn't binding on the guardian or custodian named, nor on the child, nor on any court.

6
Alimony

Alimony is the allowance awarded by a court to a wife for her own support, payable by the husband. It also refers to such an allowance made after a divorce petition has been launched, as an interim award good until trial; within the context of a divorce, interim alimony can be awarded to either husband or wife.

The award to a wife made by a Family Court is usually referred to as maintenance, so that alimony can be further defined as the award made by a superior court. The power to award alimony stems from common law, deriving in turn from ecclesiastical law of England prior to 1857 when the Church still had jurisdiction over matrimonial disputes. In this way it differs from the remedies available in a Family Court, which always derive from a statute, as explained in the chapter on Family Courts. (See Chapter 4.)

Grounds for Alimony Action

The award of alimony is limited to cases where it is

proved that (1) the parties are living separate and apart, and (2) the husband has been guilty of adultery, cruelty or desertion. If a separation agreement already exists, the wife may sue for alimony if the husband is in breach of its terms.

Often in cases where there are dependent children the wife will sue for alimony for herself, and also for custody and maintenance for the children. If so, the ordinary rules governing custody and maintenance of children will prevail; these have been discussed in the chapter on custody. (See Chapter 5.)

In Canada only a wife may sue for alimony, but, curiously enough, if a husband has been awarded alimony under the laws of a foreign country, he may sue his wife in Canada to enforce his judgment.

Defences to Alimony Action

In order to succeed in an action for alimony, an absolute requirement is a valid and subsisting marriage. No matter how badly the husband has behaved, he won't be ordered to pay alimony unless the plaintiff can prove she's his wife. As I mentioned in the chapter on marriage, this is sometimes difficult where there have been previous marriages supposedly dissolved by dubious divorces.

Sometimes a claim for alimony can be defended where the marriage appears on the surface to be valid, but an annulment is available. A few years ago I was consulted by a man whose wife had just served him with a writ claiming alimony. There was no question about the validity of their marriage in the sense that they both had the capacity to marry and had gone through a proper form of solemnization, nor was there any question that the husband had deserted his wife — he had simply walked out on her making no financial provision for her at all. But in the course of our first interview, in groping for some defence, the husband in great embarrassment told me that although he and his wife had lived together for nearly five years, the marriage had never been consummated. Apparently she had an aversion or repugnance to sex that she simply could not overcome. The lawsuit was quickly withdrawn when the wife's lawyer heard about this — his client hadn't bothered to tell him. Later the husband obtained an annulment.

Alimony is awarded on the basis of financial need. This means simply that if the wife has income and assets sufficient to maintain herself, the court will either refuse to award alimony, or will perhaps make a nominal award, regardless of the husband's conduct.

Why Sue for Alimony?

In our time, when many wives work and earn enough to maintain themselves, alimony actions are relatively uncommon. Also, many women find the idea of claiming alimony distasteful, as a reflection of women's traditional dependence and "inferior" status. Furthermore, a money award for the wife can probably be more easily obtained within the context of a divorce petition, where the governing rules are far less rigid and technical than they are in alimony actions.

So why sue for alimony at all? Well, for those who are prohibited by religion from getting a divorce, an action for alimony may produce the needed money without dissolving the marriage. An alimony action can also be used where the parties have separated, but the wife doesn't want a final break to occur (although this motive is more emotional than practical, in my view). Sometimes an action for alimony is used where the wife just won't petition for divorce, out of spite. This kind of punitive behaviour was fairly common before the present Divorce Act came into force: the only ground for divorce was adultery, and as long as the wife didn't commit adultery, there was nothing the husband could do to dissolve the marriage, even though he might be living with another woman. The new Divorce Act provides grounds for dissolution of marriage based on periods of separation, the least of which is for three years, so the threat of withholding a divorce has lost much of its sting, and alimony actions are not as popular as they once were.

The Trouble with Alimony

Alimony actions are fraught with technical traps and difficulties. Until very recently most lawyers believed that a failed demand for "restitution of conjugal rights" — meaning, roughly, a reconciliation — was necessary before the wife could successfully claim alimony. Supposedly, this demand had to be made in writing, and, of course, it had to be made sincerely and in good faith. There were exceptions to this rule and exceptions to the exceptions, but, finally, a definitive judgment has ruled that no such demand is necessary. Just as well, too. Imagine a situation where the wife is delighted to be rid of the husband because of his abominable conduct, but in accordance with legal requirements she demands his return, and, to her horror, he comes back.

It's pretty difficult for a wife who isn't working and has young children to just pack up and move out. If her husband is the sole or partial owner of the house or signed the lease, it's very difficult to force him out of the matrimonial home by any legal process. About all the wife can do is apply for an injunction, a court order restraining the husband from entering the home. If the husband has been guilty of cruelty *and* desertion, she has some chance of obtaining the injunction, on the authority of the one and only reported Canadian decision which covers this point.

Where the wife wants to live apart from the husband in order to establish her right to claim alimony, she'll usually have to raise enough money to resettle and maintain herself at least until an interim order for alimony can be obtained, and the funds start flowing. Often welfare authorities will assist the wife to do this. But sometimes it's just impossible for the wife either to move out or to force her husband out of the home. The law recognizes this reality, so that it has been held that husband and wife may be living separate and apart, although under the same roof. The court will look for evidence of financial inability to move out, together with a termination of the marriage relationship in all respects. This doesn't mean merely that the husband and wife have stopped sleeping together, but that, for example, the wife is not cooking for the husband nor carrying out any other "domestic duties", nor going out with the husband socially.

Interim Alimony

An award of interim alimony is another way in which the law attempts to be realistic. This application can be made as soon as the alimony action has been started. What happens is that the wife swears an affidavit setting out her financial need, which is served, together with a notice of the application, on the husband or his lawyer. The husband's lawyer is entitled to cross-examine the wife on the contents of her affidavit, and usually does so. He may also want to file an affidavit sworn by the husband to contradict or clarify the wife's affidavit, and then the wife's lawyer will probably want to cross-examine the husband. All this takes time, and meanwhile the wife isn't receiving any money. However, provided the wife moves reasonably promptly, the court will often award interim alimony retroactively, in many cases back to the date when the husband was served with the notice of the application.

Most remarkably, the court will award interim alimony without regard to the merits of the case as they may appear. It will do the husband little good at this stage to complain, for instance, that he walked out because of his wife's alcoholism and promiscuity. That may win for him at trial, but not on a motion for interim alimony. All the court will look for at this stage is evidence of an apparently valid marriage (satisfied by filing a marriage certificate and swearing that a marriage took place, even though it may later turn out that the marriage was not valid and subsisting at all) and *actual financial need.* The strict requirement for proving actual financial need is dictated precisely because the husband has little if any opportunity of defence at this stage. For the same reason, the award of interim alimony is designed to enable the wife to live "modestly and in retirement" until the trial; and she is expected to move reasonably quickly toward trial, or risk cancellation of her award. So the court will not on this application be very impressed by stories of a lavish standard of living, but will simply order an amount deemed to be necessary to ensure survival, and maybe a little more. The wife can also get an order entitling her to "interim disbursements", that is, the amount of actual out-of-pocket expenses her lawyers will need to bring the case to trial.

The application for interim alimony is a powerful tactical weapon. The wife can hardly fail to get an order if she can demonstrate actual need, and the husband is left shaking his head in disbelief that he has been condemned without an opportunity to tell his story; he may suspect that his lawyer has failed him in some way, and he loses confidence. Because of this tactical importance, plus the fact that the amount of interim alimony often seems to influence the amount of the final award ("She's been living on it for six months without starving, so I guess she can manage"), and leads in many cases to settlement, the application is frequently vigorously fought. You won't really know what I mean until you've seen the wife cross-examined at length on the necessity of her every little expenditure.

Adultery as a Ground for Alimony

Once again, the grounds for awarding alimony are adultery, cruelty and desertion, where the parties are living separate and apart. Adultery has exactly the same meaning in an alimony action as in a divorce petition, so in order to avoid repetition, it's discussed in the section on grounds for divorce. (See Chapter 7.)

Cruelty as a Ground for Alimony

Cruelty, which may be mental or physical, must be proved to a stricter standard in an alimony action than in a divorce. So we have two distinct approaches to cruelty, depending on which claim is before the court. In an alimony action the plaintiff/wife must prove that the defendant/husband subjected her to treatment likely to produce, or which did produce, physical illness or mental distress of such a nature calculated permanently to affect her bodily health, or to such treatment as is likely to endanger her reason, and that there is a reasonable expectation that such treatment will continue. This principle of law stems from an 1897 decision that set the standard that all Canadian common-law courts have followed ever since. A recent attempt to "reduce" the standard, so that it would conform to that established under the Divorce Act, was overruled in unmistakably clear terms by the Ontario Court of Appeal. For a comparison of the two standards of cruelty, take a look at the discussion of cruelty as a ground for divorce, in Chapter 7.

Cruelty is a question of fact in each case. What may be intolerable cruelty in one marriage may be unobjectionable in another, and the line of demarcation is blurred. Sure, there are cases of perfectly obvious cruelty, such as the husband smashing the wife's head with a hammer, but many cases present far more subtle and difficult problems. One isolated act of cruelty has been held to be an insufficient ground, particularly where the parties continued to live together for a month afterwards; but there the complaint was that the husband had slapped his wife. No doubt an isolated act of, say, stabbing, would not be so lightly regarded.

Mental cruelty is very often difficult to prove sufficiently to satisfy the 1897 rule. Certainly if the husband's conduct has caused the wife to have a nervous breakdown or become a patient in a mental hospital, the lawyer's job is made easier; in such a case he likely has psychiatric evidence available. But mental cruelty may exist, and often does today, in a home where the wife feels stifled, locked in, degraded, unable to grow. She feels she has to get out or be destroyed, but it will require a sympathetic psychiatrist to testify that the husband's conduct in restricting the wife's personal development constitutes mental cruelty. Furthermore, not every judge is of the view that women have any other role than housewife and attentive mother.

Desertion as a Ground for Alimony

Desertion by a husband arises where he is living separate and apart from his wife without sufficient cause, and, at least theoretically, in circumstances where she has a genuine desire for a reconciliation. I say "theoretically" because, as previously noted, a wife no longer must demand her husband's return; and anyway, the courts have been reluctant to rule that a wife must always be prepared to take her husband back, no matter how badly he has behaved.

"Sufficient cause" for the husband to leave would include the wife's adultery, cruelty or desertion of him. Her forgiveness of his misconduct — the technical term for such forgiveness is "condonation" and it means resumption of the marriage relationship with knowledge of the husband's misconduct — or an already existing separation agreement, are complete defences to an action for alimony. A wife's desertion of her husband may occur in obvious cases where she just walks out on him for no good reason known to law or for reasons not arising from his misconduct, or in more subtle cases where, for example, she persistently refuses sexual relations and otherwise fails to carry out her "domestic duties". As in cases of cruelty, the facts of each alleged desertion are critical to a correct assessment of liability and responsibility.

Duration of Alimony

An alimony judgment is always made subject to a *dum casta* clause, the very same medieval survival that we encountered in discussing separation agreements. The award is good only as long as the wife remains chaste. Perhaps that's another reason why alimony actions have diminished in popularity.

Otherwise an alimony judgment ordinarily runs during the joint lives of the parties, or until further order of the court. The judgment can be altered on the application of either party, who will be expected to show a significant change in circumstances, the exact nature of which will, like so many legal problems, depend on the facts of each individual case. Variation can even be ordered in a case where the original judgment was granted in accordance with a settlement arrived at by the parties.

Where an alimony judgment has been granted, and later the parties are divorced, the divorce court will usually consider the previous judgment and make some further order based upon it, and the circumstances with which the court hearing the divorce petition is then faced. Of course, this can result in a variation of the alimony judgment.

In a recent case, a divorce was granted on the petition of the husband without any reference at all to a previous alimony judgment, and a divorce decree contained no award of maintenance for the wife. It is a general rule that, if a divorce decree is silent as to maintenance, none may be subsequently awarded, and that a decree dissolving the marriage effectively ends the alimony judgment. But in an application by the wife to enforce her previous judgment for alimony, the decision was that the judgment had been granted, as usual, until further order of the court; and no further order having been made bearing directly on the question of alimony, the former judgment continued in full force and effect in spite of the divorce.

Amount of Alimony Payments

One of the most troublesome problems a lawyer can face is in assessing the amount of alimony that the husband is likely to be ordered to pay. Settlements are generally preferable to trials, because they're cheaper, faster, and represent the wishes of the parties, rather than an award imposed on them by a stranger sitting in judgment. A settlement need not be an occasion for rejoicing. It has wisely been said that a good settlement is one that satisfies neither party; I think this expresses the essence of compromise. Also, the wife may be much better off to settle for an amount that the husband can reasonably afford and that he will willingly pay, rather than try to squeeze out the last drop, and be faced with the continuing problem of enforcing her judgment against an unwilling and obstructive victim — a principle which in my view also applies to the negotiation of separation agreements.

Many people believe that a husband is obligated to pay as alimony a fixed percentage of his income, thought to be about one-third of the gross. This is quite untrue. The courts have steadfastly refused to articulate any such rule, and in a number of decisions have resolutely denied that it ever existed. Once again we face our old nemesis: the result depends on the facts of the individual case. The amount of alimony is in the discretion of the court, says one decision, the discretion to be exercised judicially according to established principles and upon an equitable view of all the circumstances. What principles?

Basically, the amount of alimony will depend on the standard of living and station in life that the wife enjoyed prior to separation, filtered through the net of actual financial need. A wife who has never worked since marriage, has no income and no assets, will ordinarily be entitled to alimony in whatever amount is needed to maintain her as she had been maintained throughout the marriage. But this principle must bow before financial reality, since the court will not order an award that will effectively prevent the husband from making a new life for himself. In a situation where there clearly isn't enough money to support two households, the wife will probably need welfare assistance, in which case the husband's payments will be assigned to the welfare authorities in order to defray their expenses. Where there's lots of money, the problem of amount of alimony hardly matters. But in a large number of cases involving middle-income families, there is enough money to maintain one household rather well, and to maintain two households only skimpily. In such cases both parties inevitably suffer a reduction in their standard of living, and they might as well face it as a disadvantage of separation, although not a very good reason for staying together.

So, the court will consider the station in life and position of the parties, the property owned by each, their respective incomes and earning capacities, and then make an award that in a remarkable number of cases hovers around one-third of the husband's gross income before taxes. Please note that we are talking about alimony for the wife alone. Support for the children is quite another matter, covered in the chapter on custody and maintenance.

Tax Relief

Fortunately the Department of National Revenue provides some relief. The Income Tax Act contains sections that permit a husband to deduct from his taxable income any periodic payments of alimony or maintenance made to his wife for herself or the children, as long as the payments are made pursuant to a written separation agreement or court order, and the parties are living apart from each other. These payments will constitute taxable income in the hands of the wife.

This tax break may not be significant if the parties are at either the high or low end of the income scale, but it can make a tremendous difference in middle-income brackets. Suppose a couple with two children have split up. It is agreed that the wife will have custody of the children. The husband earns $15,000 per year before deductions. The wife has no taxable income. Before the split, the husband would take exemptions for his wife, children and himself, and would pay federal income tax of about $2,625, at current rates.

Now if the husband pays, say, $7,000 per year for the wife and children under a court order or separation agreement, he'll be left with taxable income of $8,000 less his own personal exemption, and his federal tax liability will be approximately $1,307.

His wife will have taxable income of $7,000 less exemptions for herself and the children. She can deduct $1,350 for the first dependent child while she's separated, which is a further break. Her federal tax bite will be around $720.

So where the husband had to pay tax of $2,625

while the couple were together, the combined tax is now reduced to $2,027.

It is precisely this subsidy, if that's the right word, that makes some separation agreements economically feasible for those in the middle-income group.

Enforcement

Frequently a lawyer will hear from the husband (or from the wife quoting him) something like this: "That rotten bitch will never get a cent from me. I don't care what it costs, I'd rather pay it to you [the lawyer] than her. No court can force me to pay her. I'll quit my job (sell my business) and move to Tahiti before I'll give her anything."

Bold words. Spoken in rage and hurt, they are so rarely acted out that it is almost impossible for the lawyer to take them seriously. He just notes that the Rotten Bitch Gambit has been offered, and pursues a solution disregarding it. On the very rare occasions when acts follow the words, a number of remedies are available to the wife, including freezing the husband's assets and, in extreme cases, detaining the husband by arrest until satisfactory arrangements can be made.

Courts are not sympathetic to the husband who, shortly after separation, and while a claim for alimony is pending, decides that he really has to go back to school. An award is likely to be made which reflects his earning capacity, rather than his income. As one decision puts it, the husband has an obligation to provide for his wife in proportion to his ability to do so. He may not artificially reduce his income so as to deprive his wife of alimony, but if his income is legitimately reduced (for example, by retirement), the wife's claim for support must be similarly reduced.

A judgment for alimony can be enforced as any other judgment can, by attaching assets, garnishee of wages, examination of the husband as a debtor, and by a few special methods as well. An alimony judgment can be registered against any land that the husband owns, and constitutes a sort of annuity in favour of the wife secured by the land. The husband will find it impossible to deal with the property until the alimony judgment has been removed from the title, which will necessitate his making whatever payments are owing. But note that the land in question must be held in the name of the husband; the wife can't register her alimony judgment against land owned by a company, even if the husband is the sole shareholder, unless she can convince the court that registration in the company name is just an attempt to deprive her of her rights.

A judgment for alimony or interim alimony can be enforced through the Family Court. The wife files a copy of her judgment in the Family Court, and on default, the husband will be summoned to explain his failure to pay. He can be made subject to further orders to make good any arrears, and on further default, he may find himself sentenced to a jail term for contempt of court in failing to comply with the order. Enforcement in Family Court is generally effective because the proceedings are very similar to prosecution of criminal offences, and also because the cost to the wife (barring time off work to appear in court) is nothing.

A small point, but one worth noting, is that if the husband fails to comply with an order for interim alimony, he may be prevented from defending the wife's claim at the trial, so that a result favourable to the wife is almost inevitable. Tough stuff!

7
Divorce

A divorce is the legal process by which a valid marriage may be dissolved. The term is also used to mean the judgment (properly called decree) that dissolves the marriage.

The party who starts the divorce proceedings is called the petitioner, and the other is called the respondent. There may be more than one respondent; one of them will always be the spouse of the petitioner, together, say, with a person with whom it is alleged that adultery occurred (the co-respondent).

There's a lot of misinformation around about the ease and simplicity with which a divorce can be processed. The present system places divorces, even undefended divorces, in the context of a formal lawsuit. Here's a simplified outline of the *minimum* steps in getting a typical divorce case to trial.

Proceedings Before Trial

The petitioner starts proceedings by "presenting" a

petition for divorce. Actually, two documents are needed, a petition that contains vital statistics about the marriage and any children, the grounds on which the divorce is sought, and a statement of the relief claimed; and a notice of petition that gives formal warning that a petition has been commenced, and lets the respondent know what must be done if the petition is to be disputed. In some provinces the petition and notice of petition are physically separate documents; in others, the petition and notice of petition are combined.

A petition is "presented" when a copy is filed at the appropriate court office, in the form prescribed by the rules of the superior court of the province in which the petition has been commenced, and on payment of the fees demanded for presenting a petition, currently $30.00 in Ontario. If a copy of the marriage certificate is available, it is filed with the court office when the petition is presented.

The petition and notice of petition must then be "served" on the respondent or respondents, usually by delivery of copies of these documents to the respondent(s) in person.

It frequently happens that a respondent cannot be personally served with these papers. In some cases, by definition it's impossible to do so, for instance where the ground for divorce is that the respondent spouse has disappeared for at least three years; or it may simply be that the respondent is trying to evade service of the documents. This can be solved by an application to permit the documents to be served by "substitutional service", that is, by a method other than personal service. The petitioner can obtain an order that the documents be served by delivering them to a relative of the respondent, by mailing them to the respondent, or by advertising in a newspaper that a petition has been commenced.

Sometimes, in cases where the divorce is sought on the ground of adultery, the petitioner doesn't know the name of the person with whom adultery occurred. This may arise, for example, where the wife finds a hotel receipt that clearly indicates that the husband stayed there with a woman represented as his wife, and she knows it wasn't she. In a situation like this, before starting the petition, the wife can make an application to court for permission to issue a petition without naming the co-respondent. As you might expect, the court will scrutinize such an application closely, because of the obvious potential for fraud in such a case.

Besides claiming dissolution of the marriage, the petition may also claim "corollary relief", which includes maintenance (money for the support of either spouse), custody of children and access or visiting rights to children.

In British Columbia and Ontario, if there are children of the marriage the Official Guardian also must be served with copies of the divorce petition and notice of petition. The Official Guardian is an officer of the provincial government charged with responsibility for the legal rights of children. In all divorce cases where there are children, the Official Guardian will conduct an investigation and deliver a report to advise and assist the court in matters of corollary relief affecting the children. The report must be served by mail on the respondent spouse (unless service is dispensed with by court order), and a copy of the report filed with the court for use of the judge at trial. Either party may dispute the contents of the report by delivering a concise statement of the dispute within a stipulated period after the report is delivered.

Some problems may arise in figuring out just who is a "child" or "child of the marriage" within the meaning of the Divorce Act. The definition includes any person to whom the husband and wife stand as parents, including an adopted child, a natural child of one party where the other has a parental relationship with the child, and, conceivably, a foster child with whom both parties have such a relationship. A "child of the marriage" is a child under the age of sixteen or over the age of sixteen if the child is dependent on the parties because of illness, disability or "other cause". Some battles have been fought over this definition, but now it is clear that a child entirely dependent because of attendance at school will qualify at least to age eighteen. Recent provincial legislation changing the age of majority from twenty-one to eighteen all across Canada makes it less than clear what the status of, say, a nineteen-year-old college student would be. The language of the Divorce Act seems to be broad enough to include any truly dependent child of any age: for example, a twenty-five-year-old paraplegic child. As this is written, the Supreme Court of Canada has an appeal under consideration which will hopefully clear up the status of children over age eighteen, as to their entitlement to corollary relief in a divorce.

After the petition has been served, each respondent has a specified period, usually twenty days, to deliver an "answer". This is a document that may admit parts of the petition and deny others, dispute the petition in whole or in part, and may contain a counter-petition, that is, a claim by the respondent spouse for a divorce and corollary relief. The answer and counter-petition are delivered by serving a copy of the document on the petitioner or on the petitioner's lawyer, and by filing a copy at the court office where the petition was commenced. Of course, the original petitioner has the right to deliver a "reply" to the answer and counter-petition, but that's the end of such documentation. The petition, answer, counter-petition and reply are collectively called the "pleadings".

When the pleadings have all been delivered, the case may be entered on a list of divorces awaiting trial. If no answer has been delivered, that's fine — the petition is undefended, and may be entered for trial when the time for delivering an answer has expired. The case is entered for trial by "passing a record", filing with the now-familiar court office copies of all the pleadings delivered in the form prescribed for use by the trial judge, and by paying another fee, $25.00 in Ontario. Then you await your turn for trial.

It may be necessary to get an order for corollary relief while the trial is pending. This is done by an application for "interim corollary relief", started by a notice in the prescribed form served on the opposite party or his lawyer. The notice is almost invariably accompanied by an affidavit (a statement in writing, the truth of which is sworn to by the person signing it), setting out the facts in support of the claim for interim corollary relief. The other party may file his own affidavit opposing the claim for interim corollary relief by denying, contradicting or clarifying the applicant's affidavit. Often the parties are cross-examined under oath on their affidavits by a procedure that brings both parties and the opposing lawyers face to face in the office of a court reporter. The transcripts of the cross-examinations, together with copies of all the papers filed with the court in that case, are then used to present and argue the application. Similar principles apply to an award of interim corollary relief including interim disbursements as apply to an award of interim alimony (discussed in the chapter on alimony). The only significant procedural difference is that an order for interim corollary relief may be appealed to a single judge of the Court of Appeal, instead of by the less formal methods applicable to an appeal from an order granting interim alimony; depending on the province, this may result in an appeal taking longer to be heard.

An order for interim corollary relief may also be changed in the event of a material change in circumstances prior to trial, by bringing it back for review by the court which made the order originally.

It may also be advisable to have a pre-trial examination of the parties, called an "examination for discovery", again conducted under oath at the office of a court reporter. The examination for discovery explores the evidence to be presented at trial, and is often used to secure admissions from the other side that may be useful later on. The transcript of the examination for discovery can be used as evidence at trial by reading into the trial record such portions of it as are useful, or by invoking it as an aid to cross-examination of a party whose testimony at trial differs from testimony given at the previous examination. The examination for discovery also provides an excellent method for nailing down the testimony of a party who is co-operative now, but may be reluctant to testify at trial.

Jurisdiction

In order to deal with a petition for divorce, the court must have jurisdiction to do so. In all provinces of Canada only the highest trial court of that province has this jurisdiction. In British Columbia and Ontario, judges who usually hear cases only in lower trial courts may be specially empowered to hear divorce petitions. This is a great convenience, because these judges generally hear cases within a local area such as a county, and they are more easily available to preside than judges of the higher court, who might only conduct assizes in a small town for two weeks each year.

Jurisdiction also depends on the petitioner being domiciled in Canada. In order to have Canadian domicile, the petitioner must be physically resident in Canada with the intention of making a permanent home here. The Divorce Act also establishes that a married woman has her own domicile separate from her husband's, which changes the old common-law rule that a married woman, wherever she may reside, has the domicile of her husband.

In addition, the court of a particular province has jurisdiction to hear a divorce petition if either the petitioner or respondent has been ordinarily resident in that province for at least one year immediately preceding the presentation of the petition, and actually physically resident in that province for at least ten months of that year. There has been some controversy in the interpretation of this requirement. In one case, it was held that a naval officer who was ordinarily resident in Nova Scotia, but not physically resident for ten months of the year preceding presentation of the petition because of his duties, nevertheless sufficiently fulfilled the requirements. In another case, also decided in Nova Scotia, it was held that a lake seaman who was out of the province on his job so that he had not been in Nova Scotia for ten months of the year preceding presentation of the petition did not qualify. You figure it out.

If all the requirements of jurisdiction cannot be satisfied, the petition will be refused by the trial judge, even though the grounds for divorce may be perfectly valid.

Grounds for Divorce: Matrimonial Offences

Under The Divorce Act (Canada) of 1968, the grounds for divorce are classified under two headings: "matrimonial offences," and "marriage breakdown."

The matrimonial offences exist where the respondent, in the words of the Divorce Act:

(a) has committed adultery;
(b) has been guilty of sodomy, bestiality or rape, or has engaged in a homosexual act;
(c) has gone through a form of marriage with another person; or

(d) has treated the petitioner with physical or mental cruelty of such a kind as to render intolerable the continued cohabitation of the spouses.

Adultery. Adultery has been defined as voluntary sexual intercourse of a married person with one of the opposite sex, and has become more broadly construed to include the voluntary surrender to another person of the reproductive powers or faculties of the guilty person and any submission of these powers to "the service or enjoyment of any person not the spouse". In one case, it was held that the wife committed adultery when she had herself artificially inseminated without her husband's consent.

Many people seem to believe that adultery must be proved by direct observation. This is simply untrue. The court will usually be satisfied with evidence from which adultery can be inferred, based on familiarity of the respondents and opportunity to commit the offence. That's why evidence that the respondents spent a night together in a motel will be accepted as inferential proof of adultery, especially in the absence of any denial from the respondents themselves. By the way, in a case decided about fifty years ago, the judge ruled that although the respondents spent a night together in a hotel, adultery could not possibly have occurred, because the respondent wife was menstruating!

The correct principles covering proof of adultery were established in two cases decided in 1810 and 1894. This is the kernel of the later decision:

It is not necessary to prove the direct fact of

adultery, nor is it necessary to prove a fact of adultery in time and place, because ... if it were otherwise, there is not one case in a hundred that that proof would be obtainable; it is very rarely indeed that the parties are surprised at the direct act of adultery. In every case almost the fact is inferred from circumstances which lead to it by a fair inference as a necessary conclusion; and unless this were the case, and this were so held, no protection whatever could be given to marital rights. To lay down any general rule, to attempt to define what circumstances would be sufficient and what insufficient upon which to infer the fact of adultery, is impossible. Each case must depend on its own particular circumstances. It would be impractical to enumerate the infinite variety of circumstantial evidentiary acts, which of necessity are as various as the modifications and combinations of events in actual life.

The evidence from which adultery can be inferred may arise from the petitioner's own observations, but it's preferable to have corroboration from another witness. Anyone can be a witness — the testimony of a relative or friend will do fine.

The use of private investigators to gather evidence seems to have diminished in recent years. When adultery was the only ground for divorce, and the erring spouse wouldn't reveal his or her misconduct, there was often no choice but to call in a private investigator. Today, expanded grounds for divorce and the high cost of investigators' services make this need far less frequent. Still, there's no reason why an investigator can't be used, and his testimony is as entitled to credibility as anyone else's.

The overwhelming majority of divorces are undefended, simply because both parties want the marriage ended and they have nothing to argue about. Defended divorce cases rarely have anything to do with an attempt to hold the marriage together. Rather, the fight is about money or custody of children.

Most divorces based on adultery ultimately require the co-operation of the parties. This is partly necessitated by a statutory protection against "self-incrimination" where adultery is alleged. The statute says that the parties to proceedings instituted in consequence of adultery, and the husbands and wives of these parties are not liable to be asked nor bound to answer questions to which the answers tend to show that he or she is guilty of adultery. This protection exists at the examination for discovery as well as at the trial, and will be enforced by the trial judge without the need to ask for the protection. The parties may consent to be asked such questions, and may answer such of them as they wish; but unless the person has already given evidence in the same proceedings in *disproof* of adultery, the protection holds. The effect of this is to make it difficult or impossible to *compel* an unwilling party to provide admissions needed in proof of adultery. So where a petitioner seeks to impose a divorce based on adultery on a reluctant respondent, the petitioner better have some independent evidence of adultery available at trial.

The Divorce Act says that it is the duty of the court to refuse a decree based solely on the consent, admissions or default of the parties; a decree cannot be granted except after a trial, which shall be by a judge without a jury. In this respect, a petition for divorce is different from any other type of civil litigation; if you sue someone for money and he neglects or refuses to defend, you can get a judgment by default or on application, without ever going to court. But it is impossible to get a divorce without a trial, no matter how much the parties themselves may want it.

Some judges have shown a tendency in recent years to grant a decree sought on the ground of adultery after hearing the uncorroborated admission of the respondent spouse. Although it has been ruled that the testimony of a respondent spouse confessing adultery is not an "admission" within the meaning of the Divorce Act, there is a string of older authority to the effect that a divorce should not be granted on this kind of testimony; and anyway, it depends on the attitude of the individual judge. For this reason, anyone seeking a divorce based on adultery, and wanting a trial free of hassles, had better make some other evidence available to the trial judge. Since most divorces are both undefended and co-operative in the sense that both parties want the divorce, it is usually simple to have the respondent spouse bring a corroborating witness to the trial, especially in a case where there has been a continuing relationship with the co-respondent.

Sodomy, bestiality, rape. The grounds of sodomy, bestiality and rape have been the subject of hardly any reported decisions since the Divorce Act was passed.

Sodomy means anal intercourse. Most likely, in order to be a ground for divorce, sodomy would have to be forced on the unwilling wife by the husband. Proving sodomy might be difficult and embarrassing — medical evidence would surely help. Sodomy may also be a ground for divorce if performed with someone other than the spouse, perhaps akin to adultery if heterosexual, or as a homosexual act.

Sodomy was a ground for divorce in Ontario before the Divorce Act (1968), but rarely invoked. In the only reported decision on the subject prior to 1968, the trial judge found the wife's testimony corroborated by the fact that the husband had not defended the divorce, on the remarkable theory that a person charged with such a terrible offence would naturally defend if not guilty!

The one reported decision since 1968 ruled that a certificate of conviction for sodomy in a criminal case was inadmissible in proof of the ground for divorce, but that a confession statement filed in the criminal proceedings was admissible in corroboration of the testimony of the victim. This seems like an unnecessarily fine distinction.

Bestiality has been defined as carnal knowledge in any manner by a man or woman with a beast, and is a criminal offence. Where in any civil proceeding (such as a divorce), the act complained of is a criminal offence, it must be proved to the criminal standard — that is, beyond a reasonable doubt. Probably the best way to prove bestiality for the purpose of a divorce would be to prove that the respondent had been convicted of the criminal offence.

Rape is sort of a special case of adultery, but differs procedurally, because the person raped need not be named as a co-respondent if the respondent spouse has been convicted of the criminal offence. Prove it by proving the conviction. Rape as a ground for divorce raises some interesting academic questions. Can a wife be guilty of rape? Apparently she can. There has been one criminal case where a woman was convicted of rape for assisting someone else to commit the act, by threats and by holding a weapon while the rape was carried out.

Homosexuality. There have been a few cases of engaging in a homosexual act as a ground for divorce. Oddly enough, all the reported decisions have involved female homosexuality, proved for the most part by admissions of both respondents.

Other Marriage. Where the respondent has gone through a form of marriage with another person, a divorce will be granted, probably on the implied adultery that must have occurred. Before the Divorce Act (1968) was passed, the same situation would arise where the respondent spouse had obtained a divorce in another country, invalid in Canada, and had remarried. The petitioner would prove the divorce and the remarriage (or sometimes a bigamous second marriage without benefit of an intervening divorce), and that would usually be sufficient. Occasionally the trial judge would be unconvinced that the remarriage in itself proved adultery, unless the petitioner could also prove that a child had been born to the respondents. Presumably this sort of problem has been eliminated by the present statutory provision, but there have been no reported cases on the point.

Cruelty. Cruelty as a ground for divorce has produced the largest volume of precedent and controversy. For some time after the new Divorce Act came into force, lawyers and judges were not sure just what was meant by the wording of Section 3 (d) of the Act: "cruelty of such a kind as to render intolerable the continued cohabitation of the spouses". Some thought it referred to the standard of cruelty established in 1897 as applicable to claims by the wife for alimony, and others thought it set up a new standard within the words of the Act itself. As a result, conflicting opinions and authorities abounded, and quite a few undefended petitions were dismissed on strict interpretations of the Act. A decision of the Ontario Court of Appeal in 1970 went far to resolve the difficulty, in these words:

Over the years the Courts have steadfastly refrained from attempting to formulate a general definition of cruelty. As used in ordinary parlance "cruelty" signifies a disposition to inflict suffering; to delight in or exhibit indifference to the pain or misery of others; mercilessness or hard-heartedness as exhibited in action. If in the marriage relationship one spouse by his conduct causes wanton, malicious or unnecessary infliction of pain or suffering upon the body, the feelings or emotions of the other, his conduct may well constitute cruelty which will entitle a petitioner to dissolution of the marriage in the Court's opinion, if it amounts to physical or mental cruelty "of such a kind as to render intolerable the continued cohabitation of the spouses". That is the standard which the Courts are to apply, and in the context of Section 3 (d) of the Act that standard is expressed in language which must be taken to exclude the qualifications laid down in [the 1897 rule] . . . and in the numerous other cases which have followed and applied [that] rule in matrimonial disputes. . . .

Care must be taken in applying the standard set forth in Section 3 (d) that conduct relied upon to establish cruelty is not a trivial act, but one of a "grave and weighty" nature, and not merely conduct which can be characterized as little more than a manifestation of incompatibility or temperament between the spouses. The whole matrimonial relationship must be considered, especially if the cruelty consists of reproaches, complaints, accusations or constant carping criticism. A question most relevant for consideration is the effect of the conduct complained of on the mind of the affected spouse. The determination of what constitutes cruelty must, in the final analysis, depend on the circumstances of the particular case having regard to the physical and mental condition of the parties, their character and their attitude towards the marriage relationship.

So the test of cruelty is subjective, "whether *this* conduct by *this* man to *this* woman or vice versa is cruelty", because, as one case puts it, "The same conduct may amount to abominable cruelty in one set of circumstances, to the enjoyable rough and tumble of a happy married life in another."

Many cases present facts that so clearly constitute cruelty that nobody could doubt it. A series of beatings, until the wife can take no more; a single savage attack, such as in one case where the parties had separated because of the husband's indifference, and when he came to the wife's residence supposedly to discuss reconciliation, fractured her skull with a hammer he had brought along; harassment, abuse, degradation driving the spouse to seek psychiatric help or hospitalization for a nervous breakdown: these create no legal problem. But hundreds of other marginal cases will turn on the subjective test and the attitude of the individual judge.

Cruelty sufficient for divorce has been found in these less obvious situations:

— the practice of *coitus interruptus* adversely affecting the health of the wife.

— husband's wilful refusal to recognize the wife's right to his society.

— transvestism of the husband causing continual stress to the wife.

— husband's pedophilia.

— adoption by the husband of a hippie lifestyle and use of soft drugs despite disapproval by the wife.

— husband ignored wife, neglected her medical needs and made unreasonable sexual demands.

— chronic alcoholism of the husband (although there are cases that say that addiction to alcohol is not cruelty as such).

— petitioner wife forced by her husband to engage in fellatio against her will.

— persistent refusal of sexual relations. There have been cases both ways, husband's refusal and wife's refusal, but there have also been cases where it was ruled that refusal of sexual intercourse as such was not cruelty. The successful cases have been those in which it could be demonstrated that refusal of sexual relations had an adverse effect on the physical or mental health of the petitioner.

— wife habitually and continually ridiculed the husband's sexual performance and compared him to a previous husband and lovers. On the evidence, the wife's conduct caused the husband such anxiety that the judge said, "There is little doubt in my mind that if he had not left he would have become a prime candidate for the mental hospital."

— husband's domineering, tyrannizing or abusive conduct, particularly where it causes the wife to need psychiatric help.

The fact that the respondent was insane at the time of committing the acts of cruelty is no bar to granting a divorce. Cruelty need not be intentional; a divorce can be granted where the conduct that rendered continued cohabitation intolerable was founded in delusions.

Grounds for Divorce: Marriage Breakdown

Besides the matrimonial-offence grounds previously noted, the Divorce Act provides a number of grounds for divorce under the heading "marriage breakdown". These are:

(a) Imprisonment for an aggregate of not less than three years in the five years immediately preceding presentation of the petition;

(b) Imprisonment for at least two years immediately preceding presentation of the petition following conviction of an offence for which the respondent was sentenced to death or imprisonment for ten years or more, provided that all appeals against conviction or sentence have been exhausted;

(c) Gross addiction of the respondent to alcohol

or a narcotic drug for not less than three years immediately preceding presentation of the petition, with no reasonable expectation of rehabilitation in the reasonably forseeable future;

(d) Disappearance of the respondent for not less than three years immediately preceding presentation of the petition, provided that the petitioner has no knowledge of or information about the respondent and been unable to locate the respondent during that period;

(e) Non-consummation of the marriage for a period of not less than one year, where the respondent has been unable by reason of illness, disability or refusal, to consummate the marriage.

(f) Where the spouses have been living separate and apart for not less than three years immediately preceding presentation of the petition, or living separate and apart for at least five years if the petitioner deserted the respondent.

Imprisonment. Marriage breakdown based on imprisonment rarely arises in practice. The only reported decision under this section ruled that the respondent was not "imprisoned" within the meaning of the Divorce Act while out of jail on parole.

Addiction. The language of the section dealing with alcohol or narcotic-drug addiction is so woolly as to be almost impossible of application. Who can say that there is no reasonable expectation of rehabilitation in the reasonably forseeable future? The cases under this section hold that something more than mere excessive or habitual drinking must be proved. No medical or clinical finding need be made; it is sufficient if the respondent has a gross desire or need for alcohol or narcotics, and a psychological if not physical dependency upon the effect of same. However, it would be nearly impossible to prove addiction in the absence of medical evidence. In most cases where drinking is the problem, particularly where the respondent refuses to get any help, the ground for divorce can be more easily structured in cruelty, since the habitual drinking and related behaviour are likely to render continued cohabitation intolerable.

Disappearance. Disappearance for three years is not just a special case of three-year separation, since important procedural differences will apply. Obviously, the petition cannot be served personally, so the petitioner will have to get an order for substitutional service, likely by advertising. If there are children of the marriage and the petition has been launched in British Columbia or Ontario, the petitioner will have to get an order dispensing with service of the Official Guardian's report; there is no process for dispensing with the report entirely. Finally, the trial judge will make an order dispensing with service of the divorce decree.

Separation. Most cases of marriage breakdown are based on separation for three or five years. The problems of interpretation of this section arise in determining when and whether the parties have been living separate and apart. It is clear that the period of separation must be completed before the petition is presented. One cannot start a petition after separation for, say, two years, on the assumption that by the time the case comes on for trial the full required period of three years of separation will have matured.

It is sometimes less than clear whether the parties were living separate and apart within the meaning of the Divorce Act. There are two elements to this: the spouses must be physically separated, and they, or one of them, must have the intention of terminating the marriage relationship. There are situations where the husband and wife have been held to be living separate and apart although they continued to reside under the same roof, but such cases have been subjected to extremely careful scrutiny. Mere lack of sexual relationship will not qualify; there must be a complete removal from every aspect of the marriage relationship. In the few cases where this has been successfully invoked, there was no sexual, social or domestic relationship between the parties. For example, the wife did not sleep with the husband, went nowhere with him, did not cook or keep house for him, but, perhaps, shared a residence with him through financial necessity.

The converse is that the parties can be physically separated for a long period of time, but not be living "separate and apart", because they did not intend to destroy the marriage relationship. An obvious instance might arise where the husband is posted overseas on military service.

Great difficulty has been encountered where the respondent has been confined to hospital for a long period of time. It is a subtle question, depending on the facts of the individual case, whether the petitioner may proceed after three years or must wait for five years in such a situation. Suppose the husband becomes hopelessly insane and is confined to hospital. The wife visits him for a time, and then stops. When did she form the intention to destroy

THE GUIDE TO FAMILY LAW

the marriage relationship? Did she desert her husband, so that she must wait five years before starting a divorce? Did the period of separation start when the husband entered hospital, or when the wife stopped visiting? Can she be said to have deserted her husband when he cannot know what she feels? Regrettably, the present state of the law provides no conclusive answers to these questions, but chances are that the petitioner would have to wait the full five years for a divorce, with the time probably calculated from the time her husband entered hospital.

The period during which the parties have lived separate and apart is not considered to be interrupted if they have resumed cohabitation for a single period not exceeding ninety days, in an attempt at reconciliation. However, in one case, where the parties had engaged in one act of sexual intercourse during the period, *but had not really attempted reconciliation,* it was held that the period of separation had been interrupted and the petition was dismissed!

Any separation that is mutual or consensual will enable either party to petition for divorce after three years. A separation that starts by desertion may later become consensual, for example, by the parties' entering into a separation agreement.

The parties need not mutually reject the marriage. If the petitioner has been deserted, he or she may proceed with the petition after three years, although the deserter would have to wait for five years.

Corollary Relief

A petition for divorce may include a claim for

corollary relief as well as for dissolution of the marriage, or it may claim alimony and custody of and maintenance for children, as an alternative to divorce. The alternative may be important in a situation where the petition for divorce is marginal and may be refused; in such a case, the petitioner may still come out of the proceedings with custody of the children and money for support of herself and them.

Corollary relief as such can only be ordered upon the granting of a divorce decree. If you don't get it then, you will be forever barred, except that a Family Court order for maintenance of children (not for the spouse) will continue unaffected.

It may be that the petitioner is content to rely on the terms of a separation agreement, and will not ask the court to make an order for corollary relief, but that's another matter. The separation agreement will continue as a contract between the parties, and will be enforceable in its own terms.

Insofar as corollary relief includes child custody and maintenance and access to children, it has been dealt with in the chapter on custody. Similar rules apply in divorce cases, even to the extent that the courts will not rule on the custody of children unless they are ordinarily resident in the province in which the petition is heard.

The major difference in the law governing awards of maintenance for a spouse under the Divorce Act (as opposed to an award of alimony) derives from the wording of the Act itself: the court may make an award of maintenance for either spouse if it thinks it "fit and just to do so having regard to the conduct of the parties and the conditions, means and circumstances of each of them". Of course, words like these create a tremendously wide discretion for the court.

A wife's adultery does not as such disentitle her to maintenance, nor does the fact that she left her husband, if there was good cause for her leaving, But it has been ruled that where the marriage breakdown was caused by the wife deserting her husband, and where she is not in such a state of destitution as to require the petitioner to support her for reasons of public policy, no maintenance should be awarded to her.

Because of the somewhat ambiguous wording of the Divorce Act, it was unclear for some time whether the court could award both periodic payments of maintenance and a lump sum payment. Recent decisions make it clear that the court has this power. The respondent may also be ordered to post security for payment of the award, but this does not extend to ordering that property be sold to make payment of maintenance, nor to ordering that property be transferred from the respondent to the petitioner.

A separation agreement is no bar to the power of the court to order corollary relief, but the agreement will not be disregarded lightly. In fact, there are only two reported Canadian decisions where the court has overruled or modified a separation agreement in granting corollary relief.

The Divorce Act provides that an order for corollary relief "may be varied from time to time or rescinded by the court that made the order if it thinks it fit and just to do so having regard to the conduct of the parties since the making of the order or any change in the condition, means or other circumstances of either of them". In order to succeed on an application for variation, the applicant must show some real and substantial change since the original award was made. This section has been interpreted with extreme strictness, as if to discourage a flood of requests for variance. Note that the court can only vary an order for corollary relief originally pronounced; there is no power to impose an order for corollary relief by way of "variance" if none was made at the time the divorce decree was granted.

An order for corollary relief may be registered and enforced in any superior court in Canada in accordance with the rules of that court. This means, roughly, that it can be enforced in the same way as a judgment for alimony. One exception is that in Ontario an alimony judgment may be registered against land owned by the husband, but an order for corollary relief may not. This does not apply in those provinces that have specific statutory provisions enabling orders and judgments for corollary relief to be registered against the land owned by the respondent.

Bars to Divorce

There are three bars to divorce: "collusion", "connivance" and "condonation". All of them spell trouble for the petitioner.

Collusion. Collusion is defined in the Divorce Act as "an agreement or conspiracy to which the petitioner is either directly or indirectly a party for the purpose of subverting the administration of justice, and includes any agreement, undertaking or arrangement to fabricate or suppress evidence or to deceive the court, but does not include an agreement to the extent that it provides for separation between the parties, financial support, division of property interests or the custody, care or upbringing of children of the marriage". In other words, collusion is a fraud on the court and, if discovered, will result in the petition being thrown out, and may involve the parties in perjury charges. A lawyer who knowingly presents a collusive petition runs the risk of disbarment. A petitioner who obtains a collusive divorce can never rest secure with the decree; upon discovery of the collusion, the court may revoke the decree and reopen the proceedings.

But note that collusion is something more than mere co-operation between the husband and wife to obtain a divorce. Suppose the parties are separated, and the husband is living with another woman: there's nothing wrong with arranging for testimony to be given by one or both respondents. Collusion arises where evidence is faked or suppressed, sometimes for financial considerations, not where facts are presented to the court with the knowledge and approval of all parties. Note also that a separation agreement does not create collusion, nor does any financial arrangement about paying the costs of the divorce, as long as no evidence is being bought nor defence suppressed by promise of payment.

Collusion is an absolute bar to divorce. There are also two discretionary bars to divorce: connivance and condonation. These are not absolute bars, since the court may find them present and grant the divorce anyway.

Connivance. Simply put, connivance may consist of any act done with the corrupt intention of a husband or wife to promote or encourage either the initiation or continuance of a matrimonial offence, or may consist of passive acquiescence in the offence. Suppose a husband tells his wife that if she were to enter a certain motel room next Saturday night at about eleven o'clock, she might be "shocked" to discover him there with another woman — be sure to bring along an independent witness. There may be real adultery in such a situation and therefore no collusion, but this would be an extreme and clear case of connivance; if discovered, it would likely result in the petition being dismissed. Problems may arise where, for example, the wife discovers the husband in an act of adultery, but does nothing to interrupt it. In a recent case, the wife and a friend trailed the husband and his paramour to a parking spot, where intercourse occurred in the car. The trial judge thought the wife had a duty on discovering the situation to move in and break it up, and since she failed to do so, he dismissed her petition for connivance. On appeal it was ruled that the wife had no such duty and the petition was granted.

Condonation. Condonation is the resumption of the marriage relationship with knowledge of the matrimonial offence. If the wife commits adultery, and the husband forgives her and takes her back, the adultery has (maybe) been condoned. One says maybe, because the Divorce Act says that there is no condonation if there is a continuation or resumption of cohabitation for a single period of not more than ninety days, "where such cohabitation is continued or resumed with reconciliation as its primary purpose". So if a matrimonial offence occurs, the husband and wife can stay together for up to ninety days in an attempt to work things out, without losing the grounds for divorce. This applies whatever the grounds for divorce may be. There are conflicting judgments about what constitutes "any single period of not more than ninety days". In a Manitoba judgment, it was ruled that condonation did not arise where there was resumption of cohabitation for several separate periods, if each individual period did not exceed ninety days; but in a later Ontario judgment, it was held that the Divorce Act means just what it says, so that the parties get only one chance, one single period to attempt reconciliation for up to ninety days.

It appears that mere lust will be punished. In one case, after the marital offence occurred the husband and wife had sexual relations, but *not* in an attempt at reconciliation. Result: petition dismissed for condonation. On the other hand, there are cases that rule that intercourse between the parties is not necessarily condonation; one decision (in an alimony case, not a divorce) states that mere "casual intercourse", whatever that is, does not constitute condonation. And then there is a case where the parties resumed cohabitation without any sexual relationship; there had been none for a long time while they were together, and there was none after they reconciled. Condonation was found in that case.

The essence of condonation now seems to be a resumption of the marriage relationship and the restoration of the erring spouse to the position that he or she occupied in the marriage prior to the commission of the matrimonial offence; thus condonation has become something more than sexual intercourse between the parties, although this was formerly thought to be conclusive evidence of condonation.

Connivance and condonation are *discretionary* bars to divorce in the sense that, even if they exist, the court may in its discretion grant the divorce petition if "the public interest would be better served by granting the decree". Of course, whenever judicial discretion is applicable to a legal situation, the facts of the particular case largely determine the result. There is no definitive precedent dealing with the "public interest"; but it has been invoked successfully in some cruelty cases where the wife just hung on, trying to hold the marriage together, to a point where the husband's conduct had clearly been condoned, although by the time the case came to court the marriage was hopelessly dead.

Reconciliation

There are several ways in which the Divorce Act encourages reconciliation.

In the first place, it imposes a duty on the lawyer for the prospective petitioner, "except where the circumstances of the case are of such a nature that it would clearly not be appropriate to do so", to discuss the possibility of reconciliation with the client, draw to the attention of the client the provisions of the Divorce Act designed to promote reconciliation, and inform the client of marriage-counselling or guidance facilities known to the lawyer. Naturally, in the overwhelming majority of cases, the client isn't interested in reconciliation, or else he or she wouldn't be in the lawyer's office.

But the statutory hope of reconciliation persists. At the trial, it's the duty of the judge, before he hears any evidence, to ask the parties if there's any possibiliy of reconciliation. If one or both of them say there isn't, the trial can proceed. There have been a few cases where one of the spouses wanted to reconcile, but the other was adamant in refusing to try, and it has been ruled that both parties must be willing to make the attempt.

If both parties want to try, either before any evidence is heard, or at any later stage of the trial if the judge feels there is a possibility of reconciliation, the case must be adjourned to give the parties an opportunity of being reconciled. With the consent of the parties, the judge can appoint a counsellor to help them. If, after an adjournment of fourteen days, the parties are not reconciled, either of them may apply to the court to resume the proceedings. It's very rare that a husband and wife decide in the courtroom that they want to try to work things out, and rarer still that a judge will seek to impose his view of the possibility of reconciliation on them after he has started to hear the evidence.

Where a divorce is sought on any of the marriage-breakdown grounds, the court has a duty to refuse the decree "if there is a reasonable expectation that cohabitation will occur or be resumed within a reasonably forseeable period". This provision is hardly capable of rational interpretation, and in fact there is no reported decision where it has been applied.

In addition, where the petitioner seeks a divorce on grounds of marriage breakdown, the decree must be refused if granting it would be unduly harsh or unjust to either spouse, or would prejudicially affect the making of reasonable arrangements for the maintenance of either spouse or the children. This section is sometimes invoked by a respondent where the petitioner wants a divorce after a long period of separation. A typical case might involve a wife, who is concerned that, following a divorce, she would lose any right to a pension or death benefit that she would receive if her lawful husband died before her. In one such case it was held that the wife had been sufficiently provided for by a separation agreement, while in another the divorce decree was granted provided that the husband assigned to the wife one-half of his pension benefits. A Nova Scotia decision ruled that the fact that the petitioner intended to remarry, and that remarriage might reduce his capacity to provide maintenance, was not necessarily a justifiable reason for withholding the decree.

Decree Nisi and Decree Absolute

Assuming the trial proceeds well and the petitioner is succesful, the judge who hears the evidence will grant a *decree nisi,* which must be prepared in the proper form, signed by a registrar of the court and recorded in the court files, and served by mailing a copy of it to the respondent spouse, unless service is dispensed with. In B.C. and Ontario a copy of the *decree nisi* is also mailed to the Official Guardian. The *decree nisi* (*nisi* is Latin for "unless") will state that the marriage has been dissolved subject to issuance of a final decree, the *decree absolute,* which is issued (usually) three months later, *unless* valid reasons for not granting the divorce have been brought forward in the meantime. The *decree nisi* will set out the provisions for corollary relief, if any. In Ontario it omits the name of the co-respondent in an adultery case — a considerate touch.

Court costs may be awarded to a successful petitioner, in the discretion of the trial judge. Usually costs are awarded in cases involving a matrimonial offence, but they are not generally awarded in cases based on marriage breakdown, unless there is some element of culpability in the conduct of the respondent. For example, if the separation was a matter of agreement or consent, the petitioner would not likely get costs, but might if the respondent deserted the petitioner.

In any event, the costs awarded are in accordance with an arbitrary tariff of fees established under the rules of the court, and should not be expected to cover the entire bill for fees and disbursements as between the lawyer and client.

Any party may appeal to the Court of Appeal from judgment or order other than a *decree absolute*. The Court of Appeal has a full power of review, and may pronounce the judgment it thinks should have been given at trial, or may order a new trial. Of course, it may also dismiss the appeal. Except in very unusual circumstances, the Court of Appeal will base its decision on the pleadings and evidence that the trial judge used, so that an appeal is not an opportunity to put before the court all the things one neglected to say at the trial. Furthermore, the Court of Appeal will rarely interfere with a finding of fact by the trial judge, as long as there was some evidence to support it. In effect the Court of Appeal says, "The trial judge heard the witnesses, examined the evidence and came to certain conclusions. Why should we say he was wrong?" Similarly, a result based on exercise of the discretion of the trial judge will rarely be upset on appeal.

A further appeal may be made to the Supreme Court of Canada at Ottawa on a point of law, but first, as a screening process, the appellant must obtain permission to appeal to that court.

Before the *decree absolute* is granted, any person may apply to show cause why the *decree nisi* should not be made absolute, because of collusion, reconciliation of the parties, "or by reason of any other material facts". The court may then rescind the *decree nisi,* order a further enquiry, or make any other order it thinks proper. Actually, the courts have been extremely cautious in applying this provision, probably to discourage crank applications by parties who neglected or refused to appear at the trial. In a few cases, relief has been refused where real hardship might result, for instance where the respondent wife failed to apply for maintenance at the trial, so that none was ordered, nor could ever be awarded at a later stage. The point seems to be that the courts will not allow the parties to invoke this section so as to get another shot at a more favourable result, when all the issues could have been resolved at the trial.

Typically, three months after the *decree nisi* has been granted, the petitioner may apply for a *decree absolute*. The waiting period is to permit an appeal to be filed or an attempt at reconciliation to take place: the application for *decree absolute* is accompanied by an affidavit that no such thing has happened since the *decree nisi* was granted. The *decree absolute* is generally issued routinely, by filing the necessary papers with the court office for presentation to a judge, so that a court appearance at this time is rarely necessary. The *decree absolute* is a simple one-page document certifying that the *decree nisi* has been made final.

In some cases, the waiting time for the *decree absolute* may be shortened or even eliminated entirely so that a *decree absolute* is granted at the trial. The words of the Divorce Act permit this to be done where there are special circumstances and where it would be in the public interest to do so, provided that all parties consent and undertake that no appeal will be taken from the *decree nisi*. The classic case arises in a divorce based on adultery, where the female respondent is pregnant, and she and the co-respondent want to get married before the child is born. This has been extended to a case where the child was born a few weeks prior to trial. In another case, the waiting period was shortened because the petitioner wanted to emigrate from Canada and needed her status clearly defined. However, the courts will not grant a speedy *decree absolute* merely as a matter of convenience to the parties, for instance just because they want to remarry as soon as possible.

Where the petitioner fails to make any application for a *decree absolute,* at any time after the expiration of one month from the earliest date when the petitioner could have done so, the respondent may make an application for the decree. This protects the respondent, who may want the divorce more than the petitioner, from any refusal on the petitioner's part to get a final decree, whether founded in misplaced sentiment or simple spite.

There is no appeal from a *decree absolute,* but in unusual circumstances amounting to a fraud on the court in obtaining the *decree nisi,* the *decree absolute* may be set aside and the whole divorce re-opened. This happened a few years ago where the petitioner's case was completely faked; the evidence was perjured, and the respondent had not been notified of the proceedings. In a couple of very recent cases, the courts have dealt with a situation where the divorce was properly granted because the respondent had notice of the petition and the grounds were satisfactorily proved, but some other serious defect existed. In one of these cases, the petitioner husband and his solicitor let the trial judge believe that there was no financial arrangement between the parties, although the husband had been paying maintenance to the wife, and the continuation of maintenance after divorce was under negotiation. The wife had not formally claimed maintenance in the divorce proceedings on the understanding that it would be cleared up by agreement before trial, but the husband just brought the case on for hearing, got a *decree nisi* with no maintenance ordered for the wife, and then picked up a *decree absolute*. The Ontario Court of Appeal in dealing with this case ruled that the *decree absolute* was not subject to appeal as such, and could not be revoked in these circumstances, but directed that a trial be held as to the wife's entitlement to maintenance and the proper amount to be awarded to her.

What better way to end this chapter than by direct quotation of Section 16 of the Divorce Act: "Where a decree of divorce has been made absolute under this Act, either party to the former marriage may marry again."

8
Annulment

An annulment is a judgment declaring that a marriage apparently valid in form is for some reason void in law. The result is what lawyers call a declaratory judgment: one that declares the existence of a legal fact, and as such is considered binding on the whole world, provided that the court that gave the judgment is considered by other courts to have the power to do so.

There is no question that the Divorce Act (1968) made no change in the old common-law jurisdiction of the superior courts of each province to grant annulments.

The Two Types of Annulment

There are really two types of annulment: those where the marriage is void *ab initio* (from the beginning) because the parties never had the legal capacity to marry — for instance, where one of the parties is still legally married to someone else; and those where an incapacity arises or is revealed after the marriage, but where the parties may, if they wish, go on forever in a married state — as in a case of sexual impotence, which creates a marriage that is not void from the beginning, but merely voidable at the instance of one of the parties.

The distinction between the two types of annulment is not academic. Generally speaking, only the courts of the domicile have the jurisdiction to annul a voidable marriage, while any court wherever the suit may be brought has power to annul a marriage void *ab initio*.

This may lead to tricky problems of jurisdiction, because the rules governing domicile in an annulment are not the same as those in a divorce petition. For an annulment, you have to go back to the old common-law rule: that domicile is determined by the physical residence of the husband and his intention to make a permanent home in that place. According to common law, the wife has the domicile of her husband, no matter where she may be resident. She might be living in Alberta, but if her husband is domiciled in Zambia, the courts of Alberta will not have jurisdiction to annul her voidable marriage, although they would if the marriage were void *ab initio*.

Much of the hardship that used to result from this rule in divorce cases has disappeared with the advent of the new Divorce Act, as noted in the previous chapter, but the rule continues to apply to annulment actions.

Why Prefer Annulment to Divorce?

Well, in the first place you may have no choice.

Remember, "you can't divorce people what ain't even married". No court will grant a divorce if the basic validity of the purported marriage is in question. At the very least, any decision in the divorce proceedings will be deferred until it is determined whether the parties have a valid marriage, which might then be terminated by divorce. Secondly, if a marriage is void *ab initio,* the parties will not have any financial claims against each other arising from the purported marriage. For example, if there never was a marriage valid in law, the "wife" will have no right to collect alimony regardless of the conduct of the "husband". But this is not always the case where the marriage is merely voidable, because some provinces have statutes that enable a wife to claim maintenance for herself in connection with an action to annul a voidable marriage.

Children of Annulled Marriages

The parents of children born to a marriage that is either void or voidable have the usual obligation to support their children. This can arise in very unusual circumstances. There was one case where the parties had lived together for fifteen years without consummating the marriage — each blamed the other — but there was a child of the marriage by adoption.

Grounds for Annulment

Back in the chapter on marriage we discussed

capacity to form a valid marriage. Lack of that capacity may arise through a prior subsisting marriage; absence of consent to the solemnization of the marriage; mental incapacity rendering a party unable to understand the nature of the marriage contract; forbidden blood relationship (consanguinity); or by the fact of being just too young. All of these confer a right to apply for an annulment.

Most of the cases in which a marriage is void *ab initio* arise because of a prior subsisting marriage. Some of these cases involve families torn apart by war or political unheaval. Such a case might arise where a man fled his homeland in Eastern Europe, leaving his wife and children behind. Later, in Canada, he contracts another "marriage" without bothering to determine whether his first marriage has been validly dissolved, by death or divorce. Where the new "wife" has been deceived into entering a "marriage" that is of no legal effect, she may also have a right to claim for damages for his misrepresentation and deceit, and for assault in the form of sexual relations consented to in the mistaken belief she was his wife, as well as for annulment. However, lots of these cases arise as a result of plain ordinary all-Canadian bigamy.

Absence of consent may occur where there has been duress or threats inducing the marriage. Duress implies the exertion of force which induces fear, but not merely physical force; there may be threats or terrorizing acts preventing real willingness, despite apparent consent. Fear is a necessary ingredient, whether for the person coerced or for some other person. The legal concept of duress is pretty clear and well-defined but, as you might expect, the difficulty comes from applying it to the facts of each individual case. The age, strength of character, impressionable nature and mental capacity of the person influenced, and his or her relations with those who attempted the coercion, must be taken into consideration and measured, as must the qualities and capacity for influencing and importuning possessed by the persons charged with having exerted the undue influence.

In addition, the court may grant an annulment where there has been a basic mistake as to the nature and effect of the marriage ceremony ("It's just a joke! He's not a real minister."), particularly where the parties never lived together as husband and wife.

There have been a number of cases where marriage was contracted only in order to assist one of the parties to stay in Canada as an immigrant, but where one or both of the parties never intended a real marriage to endure. There was a precedent that where one of the parties had induced the other to marry for this purpose, an annulment might be granted; but in a very recent decision that was overruled, and as the law now stands, such conduct will not render a marriage void, unless an operative mistake, for instance as to the nature of the ceremony, is also found.

Mental incapacity to marry may be found where one of the parties was incapable of understanding the nature of the marriage contract, and the duties and responsibilities that it creates. The person seeking to prove mental incapacity has an uphill fight, since there is a legal presumption in favour of a valid marriage, and also a presumption that all persons are sane until the contrary is proved.

Sexual impotence sufficient to obtain an annulment is the incurable inability or incapacity of one of the parties to have normal sexual intercourse with the other, and must exist at the time of solemnization of the marriage. An annulment isn't granted because the parties *don't* have sexual relations, but rather because they *can't*.

Permanent inability on the part of the husband to emit semen constitutes impotence sufficient for an annulment, even if he is capable both of erection and penetration. Impotence of the wife usually takes the form of an invincible repugnance or aversion to sexual intercourse with her husband. A few years ago, there was a case in which the husband applied for an annulment because his wife refused to have sexual relations with him because, as she put it, she didn't like him. Both were perfectly capable of sexual relations, and by her own admission the wife had had relations with other men prior to marriage. Result: no annulment; but in view of the principles set out above, this case was probably wrongly decided. The fact that the wife had a repugnance to sex with her husband should have tipped the case in his favour.

You may wonder how sexual incapacity can be proved. In some (rare) cases the wife is able to obtain a medical certificate in proof of her virginity, but generally the court must rely on the testimony of one or both of the parties. The court may also draw an inference of impotence arising from illness, disability or refusal to consummate, where the defendant has refused to submit to a medical examination. However, the court has no power to order a party to submit to a medical examination as to sexual capacity.

Another problem is how long the marriage must have lasted before it can be said that it's impossible to consummate. There's no definite answer to that question. But the Divorce Act goes a long way towards eliminating the problem entirely, by permitting a petition for divorce to be presented where the marriage has not been consummated and where the respondent (the party against whom the proceedings are brought) for a period of at least one year has been incapable, by reason of illness or disability, to consummate the marriage or has refused to consummate it. Also there have been some recent decisions where persistent refusal to have sexual relations with the spouse has been held to be cruelty sufficient for a divorce, but that's another matter. (See the section "Cruelty" in the chapter on divorce.)

One interesting distinction: an annulment action based on sexual impotence may be started by either spouse, but a divorce petition based on non-consummation may only be presented by the sexually capable party.

9
Property Rights

In the law of property rights, Canada is in two parts divided. There's Quebec, and there's the rest of the country.

Quebec

Although a detailed discussion of the relevant provisions of the Quebec Civil Code and its interpretation are beyond the scope of this book, here's an outline of the situation in that province.

Since 1970, the "regime" of property as between husband and wife has been a *partnership of acquests,* which lasts until and unless the husband and wife make a different deal, as they're entitled to do.

The features of the partnership of acquests are:

1. The husband and wife are separate as to property while the marriage lasts. Either is free to deal with his or her separate property as either may see fit, except that there are some restrictions

on gifts of property to third parties during the marriage.

2. When the marriage ends, by death or dissolution, part of the property of either is subject to partition, that is, physical division, or sale and division of the proceeds. Basically, the property subject to partition is that gained or acquired subsequent to and during the marriage. Property exempted from partition includes what either had before marriage, or anything gratuitously given to either during the marriage, and other specific items spelled out in the Civil Code.

3. The partnership of acquests only applies if the husband and wife haven't contracted for one of the other arrangements: *community of property* or *judicial separation of property*.

In *community of property,* the traditional Quebec regime before 1970, the husband and wife agree to hold all property jointly. On death or dissolution of marriage, either is entitled to one-half of the property, regardless of any differences in the amount brought into the marriage. The wife has no power to bind the property as security for a debt if the husband objects.

This system apparently failed utterly to meet the needs of the people of Quebec. A survey conducted in the mid-1960s revealed that about 70 per cent of all married couples had contracted out of this system by what was then called a marriage contract, but since 1970 is known as: *judicial separation of property*. This is a contract by which the husband and wife agree that they will be completely separate in ownership and control of property. In every

113

province but Quebec, this is the regime.

Prior to 1970, the choice of property status once chosen was immutable — it could not be changed. Now the husband and wife might start under a contract for judicial separation of property, for example, and later decide they want to switch to partnership of acquests. That's fine, provided that they notify and get permission from creditors and receive court approval.

Note that if the parties do not specify their choice of property arrangements as being either community of property or judicial separation of property, they will be automatically subject to the regime of partnership of acquests.

The present regime seems at first glance to be a mere compromise between community and separation, but it's a carefully reasoned approach to the problem of ownership of assets as between spouses. It solves the injustice that can arise when the parties are separate as to property (as they are in other provinces) and, on dissolution of marriage, the husband, who has been working while the wife stayed home and raised the family, claims all the property, simply because he paid for it. Obviously, if the wife hadn't looked after the children, he wouldn't have been able to work as efficiently, but in provinces where the parties are separate as to property, this doesn't matter.

Partnership of acquests may be the system of the future in Canada. It's already in force in one form or another in the Scandinavian countries, West Germany and France. The Ontario Law Reform Commission in its Family Law Project recommended

adoption of a new system very much like the partnership of acquests.

Other Provinces

In every Canadian province other than Quebec,
husband and wife are separate as to property. This
means essentially that each owns and controls what
he or she brought into the marriage or acquired during the marriage. On termination of the marriage,
the property is divided on those lines, except for real
estate, which we'll deal with in a moment.

This division of property can lead to a hell of a
fight on the one hand and hardship on the other. Who
keeps records? Who can tell whether husband or
wife bought articles during the marriage? Maybe they
both worked and pooled their earnings. Maybe only
the husband worked, so that technically, the wife
bought nothing. Perhaps the husband put his pay
in a joint bank account and the wife wrote all the
cheques. Possibly the property in question was
bought by both or given to both.

Well, it isn't as simple as it should be. The ground
rules are that each is entitled to what he or she
bought or was given; if the thing was bought by or
given to both, then they either have to find a way to
divide it physically, or sell it and divide the cash.

In each province there's a statute that provides a
summary method for dealing with disputes between
husband and wife about title to or right of possession of any property.

Real estate is a little different. Mostly, husbands

and wives hold land as joint tenants: this method gives both of them an undivided one-half interest in the whole, where neither can deal with the land without the signature of the other, and where there's a right of survivorship so that on the death of one, the other takes the whole thing, automatically. There is another method, not often used between husband and wife, called tenancy in common, where each has an undivided half interest, but can deal with it without the consent of the other, and there's no right of survivorship.

Where the home is registered in joint tenancy, and the parties split, the wife may well be concerned about her right to stay in the home, while the husband may want to sell it and get his money out. In each province, there's a statute that permits a joint owner of land to apply for a court order directing that the land be either physically divided or sold under the supervision of the court. Since it's usually not practical to divide a residential property, the order is generally that it be sold and the proceeds divided between the parties.

There is no absolute right to partition (physical division) or sale. For more than twenty years it has been settled that this right is discretionary in the court. This is a matter of relief mostly to wives, who may be left in jointly-owned homes and want to be sure that the house isn't sold from under them. The court will usually refuse to order partition or sale of a matrimonial home as long as the wife and children are occupying it, unless the husband makes reasonably equivalent arrangements for alternative accommodation. In a very recent case, the situation was turned around: the husband was in the home with the children, and the wife had left. Her application for partition or sale was turned down on the basis that his need for a home was more important than her need for the money.

If the house is registered only in the name of the husband and the wife has made no financial contribution to it, she has no interest in the property. The wife has no proprietary interest from the mere fact of the marriage and cohabitation and the fact that the property in question is (or was) the matrimonial home.

This brings up two facets of law that the wife has going for her. First there's the "presumption of advancement", which states that if the husband buys something and puts it in his wife's name, he's presumed to have intended to make a gift of it to the wife. That's why, to take a common situation, a wife is entitled to half the proceeds of sale of a jointly-owned home, even if she never contributed a cent towards the purchase or upkeep. The presumption of advancement is one-way. If the wife buys or pays for something but puts it in the name of her husband, then the "presumption of resulting trust" arises, meaning that it's presumed that the wife only intended the husband to hold the thing for her, and didn't intend a gift. Both these presumptions are rebuttable, that is, they can be overcome, but it takes pretty convincing evidence to do so. A husband who seeks to persuade a court that although he put the house in his wife's name, he never intended to make a gift to her, has a hard fight. It can be done, but the husband will rarely succeed.

One of the most vexing questions facing a lawyer in practice is "Who is entitled to possession of the matrimonial home when the marriage relationship breaks down?" One would think that the problem has arisen so often that the law would be completely settled on the matter, but this is not so. It comes down to something like this:

(a) *House is owned by the husband alone.*

There's no way in which the wife can effectively evict him, except maybe if his conduct has been so shockingly cruel that a court would restrain him from entering the house for the protection of the wife and children. Even so, it's doubtful if such an order would be available. Property rights have a way of superceding personal rights.

If the wife has been guilty of some misconduct, the husband can probably evict her. Her adultery, cruelty or desertion of him would entitle him to say that he has no further obligation to cohabit with her, and, it being his house, he can just lock her out.

On the other hand, if the husband has been guilty of some misconduct (or even if he hasn't), he's not ordinarily entitled to throw the wife and children out, or sell the house from over their heads. Part of the husband's obligation of support for his family involves keeping them housed, as long as they are entitled to live with him. The only way he can evict his family or sell the house in this situation is if he makes reasonably equivalent housing arrangements for them somewhere else.

(b) *House owned by the wife alone.*

The husband can't evict her. She can evict him if he has been guilty of matrimonial misconduct — adultery, cruelty or desertion. Since she has no obligation to maintain her husband, she can just sell the house if she wants to.

There was a case where the house was in the name of the wife alone, and she badly wanted her husband put out. He hadn't been guilty of any misconduct, but the wife had committed adultery in a relationship that was continuing and caused her to desire her husband's absence. In a decision that attracted a lot of criticism from lawyers, the court ruled that the husband, who had committed no offence known to law, had a right to cohabit with his wife, and she had a duty to cohabit with him, overriding her property right, so that the husband was able to obtain an injunction restraining the wife from interfering with his right to occupy her house.

(c) *Husband and wife own the house jointly.* It's extremely difficult for either to evict the other. Amazingly, there is only one reported Canadian decision on the subject, where it was held that if the home is jointly owned, the wife can keep the husband out only if he has been guilty of both cruelty *and* desertion.

This can lead to tremendous inconvenience or hardship. Suppose the husband beats his wife up every payday, but continues to provide for her and the children. She goes to court for an injunction restraining him from entering the house. She says she feels terrified, unsafe, she's in danger of injury. The court will grant an injunction only in a clear case where there's no alternative, and where the danger is imminent. By the time the case comes before the judge either (1) the wife has moved out so that she is in no danger; or (2) the husband has moved out so that she is in no danger; or (3) they are still occupying the same house, but the husband isn't beating her up right at that moment. In any event, it's partly his house, so that he is entitled to occupy it. Result: usually no injunction, so that the property right, the right to occupy the house jointly owned, almost invariably will supercede the right of protection.

The wife's best bet may be to charge the husband with criminal assault; if he is convicted, she can ask the court as a condition of a suspended sentence and probation to make an order that the husband must stay out of the home. Good luck.

10
A Modest Proposal

As this is written, the Divorce Act has been in force for more than four years. In this time a large body of interpretative decisions has been reported, so that many of the problems anticipated by lawyers and academics have been solved. However, we're still left with the underlying problem: whether the courts should be dealing with divorces, particularly undefended divorces, at all, and if not, should the present system be changed.

The main trouble with the present Divorce Act is that it forces anyone who wants dissolution of marriage to go through a largely fictional adversary proceeding. Remember that the Act says that it is the duty of the court to refuse a divorce decree based solely on the consent, admissions or default of the parties, and not to grant a decree except after a trial. It's already been pointed out that this makes divorce proceedings different from any other type of civil litigation.

In the author's submission, this is basically wrong, because a divorce decree *can* be refused, and sometimes is, no matter how much the parties to the marriage may want it.

Judges are not neutral. Some are stricter than others, some more technical in their approach to divorce. Every lawyer knows this. Assuming that all judges are men of essential goodwill, eager to help and serve the litigants who come before them, the differences in individual judicial approach still can and do produce different results on similar facts. One judge may frankly not give a damn if the grounds are fully made out in an undefended divorce, as long as he's satisfied that the respondent had notice of the proceedings and could have defended if he wanted to. Another judge may consider a cruelty case with all his experience and wisdom, then conclude that, although the petition is undefended, cruelty has not been sufficiently proved within the meaning of the Divorce Act and interpretative decisions to justify his granting a decree.

That doesn't mean one judge is good and the other bad. Each judge brings to the bench his own attitudes and prejudices. The judge who insists on absolute compliance with the authorities before granting a decree is doing his job conscientiously as he sees it. The judge who doesn't may be bringing the law and the administration of justice into disrepute. Unfortunately, neither approach always produces an acceptable result for the litigants who pay for and are most affected by the process.

So, quite apart from criticism of what might be called minor defects in the Divorce Act — opaque language in some sections, reconciliation provisions impossible to administer — the trouble is that divorce continues to be a part of the adversary system of administration of justice.

The adversary system demands that one party sue the other for something, and that one party is essentially innocent while the other is guilty. This means that, before a divorce can be granted, the petitioner must prove grounds that likely have nothing to do with the collapse of the marriage as such. Fail to prove the grounds, and the petitioner fails to get a divorce. The respondent may not have been quite cruel enough, or at least not cruel in a sufficiently acceptable and impressive way. The parties may have been separated for years, but a question arises whether the petitioner deserted the respondent and so should wait a few years more. None of these things have any relevance to the undoubted fact that the marriage is dead, never to be revived, and that one or both parties desperately want to be free of its legal bonds.

As long as the decision to dissolve or not dissolve a marriage is made within the context of the adversary system, individual judicial discretion will often determine the result. It is submitted that this is fundamentally misconceived. Parties should have a right to be divorced, just as they have a right to get married. The interest of the state, and thus the interest of the courts, should lean in the direction, not of granting or withholding a decree of divorce, but rather making sure that the parties have provided for the children of the marriage and for each other to the extent of their abilities. If the parties have arranged custody, access, maintenance and division of property between themselves, the courts should be concerned only that the arrangements are reasonable; having exercised a supervisory function, correcting and revising any such agreement that seems patently or latently unfair, the courts should have no discretion to refuse a decree of divorce, at the petition of one or both parties to the marriage.

What public good can possibly be served by refusing a divorce decree?

This idea isn't original. Some years ago, the Family Law Section of the American Bar Association proposed a model statute that effectively would abolish grounds for divorce. No state or province has enacted it as proposed, but in California the legislature went a long way towards it after years of consideration of divorce reform, by enacting a statute that creates only two grounds for divorce: incurable insanity and irreconcilable differences, the latter being nearly anything that causes one or both parties to want a divorce.

The A.B.A. model statute is simple enough. This is the full text of it, as it appeared in the June 1969 issue of the *Family Law Quarterly*.

Section I. Application for Divorce or Separation

Any married person or couple may file an Application for Divorce or Separation with the Court [having jurisdiction over the area in which either of the spouses resides]. In case only one spouse files an application hereunder, the other spouse shall receive notice thereof in accord with Section IX. If within one year of the filing of an Application, no Petition for Divorce or Separation has been made under Section II, the Application shall cease to remain in force; and no Petition can be made under the next section until a new Application is filed.

The Application for Divorce or Separation shall contain the names of the parties to the marriage, the date and place of the marriage, the date and place of birth of each child of the marriage, and the current residence of each party.

Section II. Decree of Divorce or Separation

a) Six months after the filing of an Application for Divorce or Separation, either spouse or both spouses may petition the court for a Decree of Divorce or Separation. If the spouses have concluded mutually satisfactory financial arrangements and custodial arrangements for their children, they may petition the court for either Decree three months after the filing of an Application.

Upon proof that the spouses have reached informed, voluntary and economically reasonable agreement on financial matters and custodial arrangements for their children, the court shall issue a Decree of Divorce or Separation, which shall include the terms of the spouses' agreement. When the spouses do not reach agreement, or whenever only one spouse appears before the court, or whenever the children object to the agreement through their representative, the court shall decide the financial and custody issues in Special Proceedings as provided in this statute, and its order shall be made part of the Decree of Divorce or Separation; provided, however, that the objections of one of the parties shall not prevent issuance of the Decree prior to a final resolution of the financial and/or custody issues.

b) In any case where only one spouse files a petition for Decree of Divorce or of Separation, the other spouse shall receive notice of said Petition in accord with Section IX. Likewise, where only one spouse appears at the issuance of the Decree of Divorce or Separation, the other spouse shall receive such notice and a copy of the Decree.

c) Whenever it appears that a spouse has not received actual notice of a Petition for Decree of Divorce, a Decree shall not be issued except upon proof by the petitioning spouse that the non-petitioning spouse has been absent, or his or her whereabouts has been unknown, for six continuous months from the time of application, time served in the armed forces excluded.

Section III. Residence Necessary for Divorce or Separation

The petition for a Decree of Divorce or Separation shall contain affidavits or other documentary evidence that one of the parties to the marriage has resided continuously within this State for one year prior to the filing of an Application under Section I. If neither spouse has continuously resided in the State for one year next before the filing of the Application, the Petition for Decree of Divorce or Separation shall be dismissed. For purposes of this section, any applicant who was domiciled in the State at the time of marriage and has returned to the State before filing the Application with the intention of permanently remaining, or any applicant who has served or is serving with the armed forces, or the merchant marine, and who was a resident of the State at the time of his entry shall be deemed to have continuously resided in this State during the time he was absent.

Section IV. Divorce After Separation

At any time not less than three months after a Decree of Separation has been issued, either spouse or both spouses may petition the court for a Decree of Divorce. Upon proof of the prior Decree of Separation, the court shall issue a Decree of Divorce. The terms of the Separation Decree regarding finances and custody of children shall be incorporated into the Divorce Decree, unless any of the parties requests to proceed as under Sections II and VII.

Section V. Effect of a Decree of Divorce

The Decree of Divorce shall restore to each of the spouses the status of being single and unmarried.

Section VI. Effect of a Decree of Separation

The Decree of Separation shall enable the spouses to live separate and apart under whatever arrangements have been mutually agreed upon or have been ordered by the court in special proceedings under Sections II and VII and shall enable them to use the facilities of the court in special proceedings to conclude arrangements regarding finances and the custody of children. The spouses' married status, however, shall not be terminated under a Decree of Separation.

Section VII. Special Proceedings and Temporary Relief

a) SPECIAL PROCEEDINGS. In case the

parties to a marriage have not agreed on mutually satisfactory arrangements regarding finances or the custody of children, or both, any party, or all parties, may, at any time after the filing of an Application for Divorce or Separation, petition the court for a hearing designed to resolve the disputes. The Court may hold a hearing regarding finances or custody of children on its own motion whenever such hearing is required or allowed under this statute. Any orders or settlements arising out of hearings under this section, except for temporary orders, shall be made part of any Decree of Divorce or Separation.

b) TEMPORARY RELIEF. At any time after Application for Divorce or Separation, the court is empowered, upon motion of any party, to order temporary custody, support, alimony, exclusion of a party from the marital domicile, and whatever other temporary relief the circumstances justify, *pendente lite*.

Such orders terminate upon the expiration of the Application, or the entry of a Decree of Annulment, Divorce, or Separation, whichever first occurs. If within one year of the lapse of the Application, a party reapplies, the orders are reinstated as of the date of the Re-application.

Section VIII. Annulment

An action to declare a marriage null and void shall be commenced and proceed with the same procedure as for a Decree of Divorce or Separation. Such actions shall be maintainable for the following reasons only:

a) *Incestuous Marriage* — By either spouse, in case the marriage falls within the forbidden degrees of consanguinity under [the relevant statutory provision].

b) *Bigamous Marriage* — By either spouse where one of the spouses, at the time of marriage, is validly married to some other person.

c) *Non-age* — By the spouse under the legal age for marriage, or by the spouse or by his or her personal representative if a minor.

Provided, however, that nothing in this section shall affect the initial invalidity of incestuous or bigamous marriages. Actions under Subsection (c) of this section must be commenced not later than six months after the spouse reaches legal age for marriage.

Financial matters and custody of children shall be decided or resolved as under Sections II and VII.

Section IX. Notice

Whenever notice is required under this chapter it shall be by personal service, in the manner required under [the relevant statutory provisions]. If the noticed party resides outside the State, or if personal service fails, the court shall order such other notice as is most likely to effect actual notice under the circumstances, and may withhold any decree until its order is complied with.

Section X. Costs

If any applying or petitioning party is financially unable to pay the court entry fee, other court costs, and sheriff's fees, and upon the filing of an affidavit to that effect with the clerk of the court, such costs shall be paid out of the general funds of the court.

There it is: no plaintiff or petitioner; no defendant or respondent.

Settle your differences and you can be divorced in three months after the proceedings commence. Three months is the time for cooling off. After that, neither spouse can prevent the other from getting a divorce decree, nor can the court refuse the decree. The parties can stay together while considering divorce; no question of condonation or connivance. They can face their problem together instead of running from it.

If the parties can't make their own deal within six months of the time proceedings are started, either can bring the matter on for hearing. The judge grants the divorce — he has no choice — but imposes on the parties an order for corollary relief and division of property in accordance with the evidence presented to him. This puts the emphasis on fighting where it really belongs. Typically a respondent husband under the present law doesn't oppose a divorce because he expects to hold the marriage together, but rather because he wants custody of the children, or refuses to pay as much maintenance as the wife demands. Fine, go fight about it in court, but under the model statute you don't have to pretend that dissolution of marriage is the real issue.

If the case hasn't been brought on for hearing within one year from the starting date, the parties have to file a new application. This means that the court has reasonably fresh data on which to base a decision, and that a pending petition can't be held over the head of the other party indefinitely.

The commentary on the model statute contains this compelling paragraph:

> The court should not be empowered to deny divorce because one spouse or a child of the marriage objects. Granting divorce, even over objection, best serves the state's goal of maximizing individual freedom. Denial of divorce means that both parties, though no longer a viable marital unit, are denied the freedom to establish new as well as residual family relationships. Granting divorce, on the other hand, frees each individual to marry or not marry, even to decide to remarry one another. This policy — that no marriage must be *maintained* without the full and free consent of husband and wife — is but a concomitant of the state's unassailable policy that no marriage can be *established* without the full and free consent of the parties.

Only Parliament has the power to amend the Divorce Act (1968) so as to reform the divorce law of Canada. In 1968 the new Act represented for many Canadians a revolutionary change; but it is not as liberal as many of its proponents wanted it to be at the time, for the Act was compromised by the strain of getting it passed over the opposition of the sizeable minority of the population that favours more difficult divorce or no divorce at all. Now it appears that the Divorce Act did not go far enough — not far enough to unburden the courts from the artificiality and hypocrisy imposed by the administration of the present divorce legislation.

Appendix A

What Your Lawyer Will Probably Want To Know

The first interview between a lawyer and a new client who has a matrimonial problem is something like the first meeting with a doctor. It's a fact-gathering session in which the lawyer is likely to ask a lot of questions to compile the history he needs as a basis for advising the client and planning tactics.

You can make it easier for your lawyer and yourself by putting together information before the first interview. The list that follows is not exhaustive by any means, but will cover a lot of the usual questions.

— The correct full names of the parties to the marriage and the date and place of the marriage. Try to bring along your marriage certificate, which contains this information.

— Addresses and telephone numbers of all parties.

— Residence addresses of the spouses for at least the past year.

— Correct full names and birthdates of all children of the marriage; information about their past, present and proposed residence, maintenance and education.

— Data about any prior marriage of either of the spouses. A certified copy of a divorce decree dissolving a previous marriage would be useful.

— Financial information about the spouses, which would include:

— Place of employment, salary, expense allowance, company car, other benefits;
— Significant assets owned by each spouse either individually or jointly, such as real estate, stocks, bonds, accounts or mortgages receivable, savings accounts, interest in an estate, income other than from employment, automobiles, boats, works of art, collections;
— Significant liabilities of each, such as mortgages payable; bank, finance-company or credit-union loans; time payment purchases, overdue charge accounts, etc.;
— Full particulars of life, hospital and medical insurance coverage.

— Information that will assist in assessing the cost of maintaining the family in its present lifestyle, e.g., besides basic expenses for food, clothing, shelter and transportation, data about special lessons or tuition for the children; special health problems that need regular medication or treatment; tithes or church memberships; club dues; travel or vacation habits; hobbies. At some stage you may be asked to prepare a budget setting out estimated monthly expenses for the family; this could usefully be done before the first interview.

— Dates of any previous separation.

— Particulars of any previous legal proceedings between husband and wife or involving any of the children.

— Information about any separation or financial

agreements between the parties. If you already have a separation agreement, don't forget to bring it along.

— If the concern is adultery, as much information as possible about where, when and with whom the adultery occurred.

— If the problem is cruelty, dates and places where it occurred; where and when any medical treatment was obtained; whether the police were ever involved, and if so, dates and places of any conviction; details of psychiatric treatment for either spouse during the marriage.

— Information about any attempts at reconciliation or marriage counselling.

Appendix B

The Divorce Act (Canada)

16 ELIZABETH II

CHAP. 24

An Act respecting Divorce

[Assented to 1 February, 1968]

Her Majesty, by and with the advice and consent of the Senate and House of Commons of Canada, enacts as follows:

SHORT TITLE

1. This Act may be cited as the *Divorce Act.* Short title

INTERPRETATION

2. In this Act,

(a) "child" of a husband and wife includes any person to whom the husband and wife stand *in loco parentis* and any person of whom either of the husband or the wife is a parent and to whom the other of them stands *in loco parentis;* — Definitions "Child"

(b) "children of the marriage" means each child of a husband and wife who at the material time is — "Children of the marriage"

  (i) under the age of sixteen years, or

  (ii) sixteen years of age or over and under their charge but unable, by reason of illness, disability or other cause, to withdraw himself from their charge or to provide himself with necessaries of life;

(c) "collusion" means an agreement or conspiracy to which a petitioner is either directly or indirectly a party for the purpose of subverting the administration of justice, and includes any agreement, understanding or arrangement to fabricate or suppress evidence or to deceive the court, but does not include an agreement to the — "Collusion"

THE GUIDE TO FAMILY LAW

extent that it provides for separation
between the parties, financial support,
division of property interests or the
custody, care or upbringing of children of the marriage;

"Condonation"

(d) "condonation" does not include the
continuation or resumption of cohabitation during any single period
of not more than ninety days, where
such cohabitation is continued or resumed with reconciliation as its primary purpose;

"Court"

(e) "court" for any province means,

(i) for the Province of Ontario, Nova
Scotia, New Brunswick or Alberta, the trial division or branch
of the Supreme Court of the
Province,

(ii) for the Province of Quebec,

(A) where no proclamation has
been issued under subsec-
tion (1) of section 22, the
Divorce Division of the Exchequer Court, or

(B) where a proclamation has
been issued under subsec-
tion (1) of section 22, the
Superior Court of the Province,

(iii) for the Province of Newfoundland,

(A) where no proclamation has
been issued under subsec-
tion (2) of section 22, the
Divorce Division of the Exchequer Court, or

(B) where a proclamation has
been issued under subsec-
tion (2) of section 22, the
Supreme Court of the Province,

     (iv) for the Province of British Columbia or Prince Edward Island, the Supreme Court of the Province,

     (v) for the Province of Manitoba or Saskatchewan, the Court of Queen's Bench for the Province, and

     (vi) for the Yukon Territory or the Northwest Territories, the Territorial Court thereof;

  (*f*) "court of appeal" means   *"Court of appeal"*

     (i) with respect to an appeal from a court other than the Divorce Division of the Exchequer Court, the court exercising general appellate jurisdiction with respect to appeals from that court, and

     (ii) with respect to an appeal from the Divorce Division of the Exchequer Court, the Exchequer Court of Canada; and

  (*g*) "petition" for divorce means a petition or motion for a decree of divorce, either with or without corollary relief by way of an order under section 10 or 11.   *"Petition"*

GROUNDS FOR DIVORCE

3. Subject to section 5, a petition for divorce *Grounds* may be presented to a court by a husband or wife, on the ground that the respondent, since the celebration of the marriage,

  (*a*) has committed adultery;

  (*b*) has been guilty of sodomy, bestiality or rape, or has engaged in a homosexual act;

  (*c*) has gone through a form of marriage with another person; or

  (*d*) has treated the petitioner with physical or mental cruelty of such a kind as to render intolerable the continued cohabitation of the spouses.

Additional grounds

4. (1) In addition to the grounds specified in section 3, and subject to section 5, a petition for divorce may be presented to a court by a husband or wife where the husband and wife are living separate and apart, on the ground that there has been a permanent breakdown of their marriage by reason of one or more of the following circumstances as specified in the petition, namely:

(a) the respondent

    (i) has been imprisoned, pursuant to his conviction for one or more offences, for a period or an aggregate period of not less than three years during the five-year period immediately preceding the presentation of the petition, or

    (ii) has been imprisoned for a period of not less than two years immediately preceding the presentation of the petition pursuant to his conviction for an offence for which he was sentenced to death or to imprisonment for a term of ten years or more, against which conviction or sentence all rights of the respondent to appeal to a court having jurisdiction to hear such an appeal have been exhausted;

(b) the respondent has, for a period of not less than three years immediately preceding the presentation of the petition, been grossly addicted to alcohol, or a narcotic as defined in the *Narcotic Control Act*, and there is no reasonable expectation of the respondent's rehabilitation within a reasonably foreseeable period;

(c) the petitioner, for a period of not less than three years immediately preceding the presentation of the petition, has had no knowledge of or information as to the whereabouts of the respondent and, throughout that period, has been unable to locate the respondent;

(d) the marriage has not been consummated and the respondent, for a period of not less than one year, has been unable by reason of illness or disability to consummate the marriage, or has refused to consummate it; or

(e) the spouses have been living separate and apart
  (i) for any reason other than that described in subparagraph (ii), for a period of not less than three years, or
  (ii) by reason of the petitioner's desertion of the respondent, for a period of not less than five years,
immediately preceding the presentation of the petition.

(2) On any petition presented under this section, where the existence of any of the circumstances described in subsection (1) has been established, a permanent breakdown of the marriage by reason of those circumstances shall be deemed to have been established. *Where circumstances established*

JURISDICTION OF COURT

5. (1) The court for any province has jurisdiction to entertain a petition for divorce and to grant relief in respect thereof if, *Jurisdiction to entertain petition*

(a) the petition is presented by a person domiciled in Canada; and

(b) either the petitioner or the respondent has been ordinarily resident in that province for a period of at least one year immediately preceding the presentation of the petition and has actually resided in that province for at least ten months of that period.

Where petition pending before two courts

(2) Where petitions for divorce are pending between a husband and wife before each of two courts that would otherwise have jurisdiction under this Act respectively to entertain them and to grant relief in respect thereof,

(a) if the petitions were presented on different days and the petition that was presented first is not discontinued within thirty days after the day it was presented, the court to which a petition was first presented has exclusive jurisdiction to grant relief between the parties and the other petition shall be deemed to be discontinued; and

(b) if the petitions were presented on the same day and neither of them is discontinued within thirty days after that day, the Divorce Division of the Exchequer Court has exclusive jurisdiction to grant relief between the parties and the petition or petitions pending before the other court or courts shall be removed, by direction of the Divorce Division of the Exchequer Court, into that Court for adjudication.

Where petition opposed

(3) Where a husband or wife opposes a petition for divorce, the court may grant to such spouse the relief that might have been granted to him or to her if he or she had presented a petition to the court seeking that relief and the court had had jurisdiction to entertain the petition under this Act.

DOMICILE

6. (1) For all purposes of establishing the jurisdiction of a court to grant a decree of divorce under this Act, the domicile of a married woman shall be determined as if she were unmarried and, if she is a minor, as if she had attained her majority.

Rule for determining domicile

(2) For all purposes of determining the marital status in Canada of any person and without limiting or restricting any existing rule of law applicable to the recognition of decrees of divorce granted otherwise than under this Act, recognition shall be given to a decree of divorce, granted after the coming into force of this Act under a law of a country or subdivision of a country other than Canada by a tribunal or other competent authority that had jurisdiction under that law to grant the decree, on the basis of the domicile of the wife in that country or subdivision determined as if she were unmarried and, if she was a minor, as if she had attained her majority.

Recognition of foreign decrees based on wife's domicile

PRESENTATION AND HEARING OF PETITIONS:

SPECIAL DUTIES

7. (1) It shall be the duty of every barrister, solicitor, lawyer or advocate who undertakes to act on behalf of a petitioner or a respondent on a petition for divorce under this Act, except where the circumstances of the case are of such a nature that it would clearly not be appropriate to do so,

Duty of legal adviser respecting possibility of reconciliation

  (a) to draw to the attention of his client those provisions of this Act that have as their object the effecting where possible of the reconciliation of the parties to a marriage;

  (b) to inform his client of the marriage counselling or guidance facilities known to him that might endeavour to assist the client and his or her spouse with a view to their possible reconciliation; and

(*c*) to discuss with his client the possibility of the client's reconciliation with his or her spouse.

Statement to be endorsed on petition

(2) Every petition for divorce that is presented to a court by a barrister, solicitor, lawyer or advocate on behalf of a petitioner shall have endorsed thereon a statement by such barrister, solicitor, lawyer or advocate certifying that he has complied with the requirements of this section.

Reconciliation proceedings

8. (1) On a petition for divorce it shall be the duty of the court, before proceeding to the hearing of the evidence, to direct such inquiries to the petitioner and, where the respondent is present, to the respondent as the court deems necessary in order to ascertain whether a possibility exists of their reconciliation, unless the circumstances of the case are of such a nature that it would clearly not be appropriate to do so, and if at that or any later stage in the proceedings it appears to the court from the nature of the case, the evidence or the attitude of the parties or either of them that there is a possibility of such a reconciliation, the court shall

(*a*) adjourn the proceedings to afford the parties an opportunity of becoming reconciled; and

(*b*) with the consent of the parties or in the discretion of the court, nominate
  (i) a person with experience or training in marriage counselling or guidance, or
  (ii) in special circumstances, some other suitable person,

to endeavour to assist the parties with a view to their possible reconciliation.

Resumption of hearing

(2) Where fourteen days have elapsed from the date of any adjournment under sub-

section (1) and either of the parties applies to the court to have the proceedings resumed, the court shall resume the proceedings.

ADDITIONAL DUTIES OF COURT

9. (1) On a petition for divorce it shall be the duty of the court

Duty of court on petition

(a) to refuse a decree based solely upon the consent, admissions or default of the parties or either of them, and not to grant a decree except after a trial which shall be by a judge, without a jury;

(b) to satisfy itself that there has been no collusion in relation to the petition and to dismiss the petition if it finds that there was collusion in presenting or prosecuting it;

(c) where a decree is sought under section 3, to satisfy itself that there has been no condonation or connivance on the part of the petitioner, and to dismiss the petition if the petitioner has condoned or connived at the act or conduct complained of unless, in the opinion of the court, the public interest would be better served by granting the decree;

(d) where a decree is sought under section 4, to refuse decree if there is a reasonable expectation that cohabitation will occur or be resumed within a reasonably foreseeable period;

(e) where a decree is sought under section 4, to refuse the decree if there are children of the marriage and the granting of the decree would prejudicially affect the making of reasonable arrangements for their maintenance; and

(f) where a decree is sought under section 4 by reason of circumstances described in paragraph (e) of subsection (1) of that section, to refuse the decree if the granting of the decree would be unduly harsh or unjust to either spouse or would prejudicially affect the making of such reasonable arrangements for the maintenance of either spouse as are necessary in the circumstances.

Revival

(2) Any act or conduct that has been condoned is not capable of being revived so as to constitute a ground for divorce described in section 3.

Calculation of period of separation

(3) For the purposes of paragraph (e) of subsection (1) of section 4, a period during which a husband and wife have been living separate and apart shall not be considered to have been interrupted or terminated

(a) by reason only that either spouse has become incapable of forming or having an intention to continue to live so separate and apart or of continuing to live so separate and apart of his or her own volition, if it appears to the court that the separation would probably have continued if such spouse had not become so incapable; or

(b) by reason only that there has been a resumption of cohabitation by the spouses during a single period of not more than ninety days with reconciliation as its primary purpose.

COROLLARY RELIEF

Interim orders

10. Where a petition for divorce has been presented, the court having jurisdiction to grant relief in respect thereof may make such interim orders as it thinks fit and just

(a) for the payment of alimony or an

alimentary pension by either spouse for the maintenance of the other pending the hearing and determination of the petition, accordingly as the court thinks reasonable having regard to the means and needs of each of them;

(*b*) for the maintenance of and the custody, care and upbringing of the children of the marriage pending the hearing and determination of the petition; or

(*c*) for relieving either spouse of any subsisting obligation to cohabit with the other.

11. (1) Upon granting a *decree nisi* of divorce, the court may, if it thinks it fit and just to do so having regard to the conduct of the parties and the condition, means and other circumstances of each of them, make one or more of the following orders, namely:

Orders granting corollary relief

(*a*) an order requiring the husband to secure or to pay such lump sum or periodic sums as the court thinks reasonable for the maintenance of both or either
  (i) the wife, and
  (ii) the children of the marriage;

(*b*) an order requiring the wife to secure or to pay such lump sum or periodic sums as the court thinks reasonable for the maintenance of both or either
  (i) the husband, and
  (ii) the children of the marriage; and

(*c*) an order providing for the custody, care and upbringing of the children of the marriage.

(2) An order made pursuant to this section may be varied from time to time or rescinded by the court that made the order if it thinks it fit and just to do so having regard to

Variation, etc., of order granting corollary relief

the conduct of the parties since the making of the order or any change in the condition, means or other circumstances of either of them.

Payment and conditions

12. Where a court makes an order pursuant to section 10 or 11, it may

(a) direct that any alimony, alimentary pension or maintenance be paid either to the husband or wife, as the case may be, or to a trustee or administrator approved by the court; and

(b) impose such terms, conditions or restrictions as the court thinks fit and just.

DECREES AND ORDERS

Decree nisi

13. (1) Every decree of divorce shall in the first instance be a *decree nisi* and no such decree shall be made absolute until three months have elapsed from the granting of the decree and the court is satisfied that every right to appeal from the judgment granting the decree has been exhausted.

Special circumstances

(2) Notwithstanding subsection (1), where, upon or after the granting of a *decree nisi* of divorce,

(a) the court is of opinion that by reason of special circumstances it would be in the public interest for the decree to be made absolute before the time when it could be made absolute under subsection (1), and

(b) the parties agree and undertake that no appeal will be taken, or any appeal that has been taken has been abandoned,

the court may fix a shorter time after which the decree may be made absolute or, in its discretion, may then make the decree absolute.

Cause may be shown

(3) Where a *decree nisi* of divorce has been granted but not made absolute, any per-

son may show cause to the court why the decree should not be made absolute, by reason of its having been obtained by collusion, by reason of the reconciliation of the parties or.by reason of any other material facts, and in any such case the court may by order,

> (a) rescind the *decree nisi*;
>
> (b) require further inquiry to be made; or
>
> (c) make such further order as the court thinks fit.

(4) Where a *decree nisi* of divorce has been granted by a court and no application has been made by the party to whom the decree was granted to have it made absolute, then, at any time after the expiration of one month from the earliest date on which that party could have made such an application, the party against whom it was granted may apply to the court to have the decree made absolute and, subject to any order made under subsection (3), the court may then make the decree absolute. *Where decree not made absolute*

14. A decree of divorce granted under this Act or an order made under section 10 or 11 has legal effect throughout Canada. *Effect of decree or order*

15. An order made under section 10 or 11 by any court may be registered in any other superior court in Canada and may be enforced in like manner as an order of that superior court or in such other manner as is provided for by any rules of court or regulations made under section 19. *Registration and enforcement of orders*

16. Where a decree of divorce has been made absolute under this Act, either party to the former marriage may marry again. *Decree absolute*

Appeals

17. (1) Subject to subsection (3), an appeal lies to the court of appeal from a judgment or *Appeal to court of appeal*

order, whether final or interlocutory, other than a decree absolute, pronounced by a court under this Act.

Powers of court of appeal

(2) The court of appeal may

(a) dismiss the appeal; or

(b) allow the appeal and

    (i) pronounce the judgment that ought to have been pronounced including such order or such further or other order as it deems just, or

    (ii) order a new trial where it deems it necessary to do so to correct a substantial wrong or miscarriage of justice.

Notice of appeal

(3) An appeal under subsection (1) shall be brought by filing a notice of appeal in the court of appeal not later than fifteen days after the pronouncing of the judgment or the making of the order being appealed from.

Extension of time

(4) Except where a decree of divorce has been made absolute, the court of appeal or a judge thereof may, on special grounds, either before or after the expiration of the time fixed by subsection (3) for bringing an appeal, by order extend that time.

Appeal to Supreme Court of Canada

18. (1) An appeal lies on a question of law to the Supreme Court of Canada with leave of that court from a decision of the court of appeal under section 17.

Leave to Appeal

(2) Leave to appeal under this section may be granted within thirty days from the pronouncing of the judgment or order being appealed from or within such extended time as the Supreme Court of Canada or a judge thereof may, before the expiration of those thirty days, fix or allow.

RULES OF COURT

19. (1) A court or court of appeal may make rules of court applicable to any proceedings under this Act within the jurisdiction of that court, including, without restricting the generality of the foregoing, rules of court

Rules of court

    (*a*) regulating the pleading, practice and procedure in the court, including the addition of persons as parties to the proceedings;

    (*b*) regulating the sittings of the court;

    (*c*) respecting the fixing and awarding of costs;

    (*d*) providing for the registration and enforcement of orders made under this Act including their enforcement after death; and

    (*e*) prescribing and regulating the duties of officers of the court and any other matter considered expedient to attain the ends of justice and carry into effect the purposes and provisions of this Act.

(2) Notwithstanding subsection (1), the Governor in Council may make such regulations as he considers proper to assure uniformity in the rules of court made under this Act, and any regulations made under this subsection prevail over rules of court made under subsection (1).

Regulations

(3) The provisions of any law or of any rule of court, regulation or other instrument made thereunder respecting any matter in relation to which rules of court may be made under subsection (1), that were in force in Canada or any province immediately before the coming into force of this Act and that are not inconsistent with this Act, continue in force as though enacted or made by or under this Act at such time as they are altered by rules of

Continuation of procedural laws

court or regulations made under this section or are, by virtue of the making of any rules of court or regulations under this section, rendered inconsistent with those rules or regulations.

EVIDENCE

Provincial laws of evidence

20. (1) Subject to this or any other Act of the Parliament of Canada, the laws of evidence of the province in which any proceedings under this Act are taken, including the laws of proof of service of any petition or other document, apply to such proceedings.

Where proceedings deemed taken

(2) For the purposes of this section,

(a) where any proceedings under this Act are taken before the Divorce Division of the Exchequer Court as the court for any province, the proceedings shall be deemed to be taken in that proince; and

(b) where any petitions for divorce pending between a husband and wife are removed under subsection (2) of section 5 by direction of the Divorce Division of the Exchequer Court into that Court for adjudication, the proceedings shall be deemed to be taken in the province specified in such direction to be the province with which the husband and wife are or have been most closely associated according to the facts appearing from the petitions.

Admissions and communications made in course of reconciliation proceedings

21. (1) A person nominated by a court under this Act to endeavour to assist the parties to a marriage with a view to their possible reconciliation is not competent or compellable in any legal proceedings to disclose any admission or communication made to him in his capacity as the nominee of the court for that purpose.

Idem

(2) Evidence of anything said or of any

admission or communication made in the course of an endeavour to assist the parties to a marriage with a view to their possible reconciliation is not admissible in any legal proceedings.

QUEBEC AND NEWFOUNDLAND COURTS

22. (1) The Governor in Council may, on the recommendation of the Lieutenant Governor in Council of Quebec, issue a proclamation declaring the Superior Court of Quebec to be the court for that Province for the purposes of this Act, and on or after the issue of such proclamation any petition for divorce presented under section 3 or 4 that would, if it had been presented after the coming into force of this Act but before the issue of the proclamation, have been presented to the Divorce Division of the Exchequer Court as the court for that Province, shall be presented to the Superior Court of Quebec.

Proclamation respecting Superior Court of Quebec

(2) The Governor in Council may, on the recommendation of the Lieutenant Governor in Council of Newfoundland, issue a proclamation declaring the Supreme Court of Newfoundland to be the court for that Province for the purposes of this Act, and on or after the issue of such proclamation any petition for divorce presented under section 3 or 4 that would, if it had been presented after the coming into force of this Act but before the issue of the proclamation, have been presented to the Divorce Division of the Exchequer Court as the court for that Province, shall be presented to the Supreme Court of Newfoundland.

Proclamation respecting Supreme Court of Newfoundland

(3) Subject to subsection (4) but notwithstanding any other provision of this Act, where a proclamation has been issued under subsection (1) or (2) a petition for divorce presented to the Divorce Division of the Exchequer Court before the proclamation was issued shall be dealt with and disposed of as if the proclamation had not been issued.

Petition previously presented to Divorce Division of Exchequer Court

Variation
of order made
by Divorce
Division of
Exchequer
Court

(4) Where a decree of divorce has been granted by the Divorce Division of the Exchequer Court

    (*a*) after the coming into force of this Act but before the issue of a proclamation referred to in subsection (3), or

    (*b*) pursuant to subsection (3),

any order made pursuant to subsection (1) of section 11 may be varied from time to time or rescinded pursuant to subsection (2) of that section by the court that would have had jurisdiction to grant the decree of divorce corollary to which the order was made if the proclamation had been issued at the time when the petition for the decree was presented and that court had made the order by way of corollary relief in respect of a petition presented to it.

CONSEQUENTIAL AMENDMENTS

R.S., c. 98

23. (1) The *Exchequer Court Act* is amended by adding thereto, immediately after section 4 thereof, the following sections:

Divorce
Division

"4A. (1) A division of the Exchequer Court called the Divorce Division is hereby established.

Constitution
of Divorce
Division

(2) The Divorce Division shall consist of the following regular judges:

    (*a*) the judge of the Court who was designated under section 6A to exercise and perform the powers, duties and functions of the officer of the Senate referred to in section 3 of the *Dissolution and Annulment of Marriages Act*, and

    (*b*) such other judges of the Court as may, in the instruments authorizing their appointment, be designated as judges of the Divorce Division.

Ex officio
judges

(3) Notwithstanding subsection (2), the President of the Court is *ex officio* Presi-

dent of the Divorce Division and each of the puisne judges is *ex officio* a judge of the Divorce Division, and as such have and may exercise in all respects, the same jurisdiction as regular judges of the Divorce Division.

(4) The Registrar of the Court is *ex officio* the Registrar of the Divorce Division.   Registrar

4B. Subject to the rules of court and except as otherwise provided by any order made by the Governor in Council, any judge of the Divorce Division may sit and act at any time and at any place in Canada for the transaction of the business of the Divorce Division or any part thereof."   Sittings

(2) Section 8 of the said Act is repealed and the following substituted therefor:

"8. (1) Subject to subsection (3) any judge of a superior court or county court in Canada, and any person who has held office as a judge of a superior court or county court in Canada, may, at the request of the President made with the approval of the Governor in Council, sit and act as a judge of the Exchequer Court and as a judge of the Divorce Division.   Persons qualified to sit and act as judge

(2) No request may be made under subsection (1) to a judge of a provincial court without the consent of the Attorney General of that province.   Consent of Attorney General

(3) The Governor in Council may approve the making of requests pursuant to subsection (1) either specifically or in general terms, and for particular periods or purposes, and in approving in general terms any such request may limit the number of persons who may sit and act pursuant to any request.   Approval of Governor in Council

(4) A person who sits and acts as a judge pursuant to subsection (1) shall be   Remuneration while acting

paid a salary for the period he so sits and acts at the rate fixed by the *Judges Act* for puisne judges of the Exchequer Court less any amount otherwise payable to him under that Act in respect of that period."

(3) Section 33 of the said Act is amended by adding thereto the following subsection:

Quorum
for appeals
under
Divorce Act

"(2) Notwithstanding subsection (1), not less than three judges of the Exchequer Court shall sit and act on the hearing and determination of any appeal to the Exchequer Court under section 17 of the *Divorce Act*, but in no case shall a judge who has heard a petition for divorce sit and act on the hearing and determination of any appeal under that section from a judgment or order in respect of that petition."

R.S., c. 176

24. (1) The long title to the *Marriage and Divorce Act* is repealed and the following substituted therefor:
"An Act respecting Marriage"

(2) Section 1 of the said Act is repealed and the following substituted therefor:

Short
title

"1. This Act may be cited as the *Marriage Act*."

(3) The heading preceding section 4 and sections 4 to 6 of the said Act are repealed.

TRANSITIONAL AND REPEAL

Petition
presented
after commencement
of Act

25. (1) A petition for divorce presented in Canada after the coming into force of this Act shall be governed and regulated by this Act, whether or not the material facts or circumstances giving rise to the petition occurred wholly or partly before the coming into force of this Act.

Where
proceedings
or petition
previously
commenced

(2) Notwithstanding the repeal by section 26 of the Acts and laws referred to in that section but subject to subsection (3) of this section,

(a) any proceedings for divorce commenced in any court in Canada of competent jurisdiction before the coming into force of this Act and not finally disposed of when this Act comes into force, shall be dealt with and disposed of in accordance with the law as it was immediately before the coming into force of this Act, as though that law had not been repealed; and

(b) any petition for the dissolution or annulment of a marriage filed under the *Dissolution and Annulment of Marriages Act* before the coming into force of this Act and not finally disposed of when this Act comes into force shall be dealt with and disposed of in accordance with that Act, as though that Act had not been repealed.

(3) Where a decree of divorce has been granted before the coming into force of this Act or pursuant to subsection (2), any order to the effect described in subsection (1) of section 11 may be varied from time to time or rescinded in accordance with subsection (2) of that section by the court that would have had jurisdiction to grant the decree of divorce corollary to which the order was made if this Act had been in force at the time when the petition for the decree was presented and that court had made the order by way of corollary relief in respect of a petition presented to it. *Variation of order previously made*

26. (1) The *Dissolution and Annulment of Marriages Act*, the *Divorce Jurisdiction Act*, the *Divorce Act (Ontario)*, in so far as it relates to the dissolution of marriage, and the *British Columbia Divorce Appeals Act* are repealed. *Repeal*

(2) Subject to subsection (3) of section 19, all other laws respecting divorce that were in force in Canada or any province immedi- *Idem*

ately before the coming into force of this Act are repealed, but nothing in this Act shall be construed as repealing any such law to the extent that it constitutes authority for any other matrimonial cause.

COMMENCEMENT

Coming into force

27. This Act shall come into force on such day not earlier than three months after the date this Act is assented to as may be fixed by proclamation.

Appendix C

Where to Write for Marriage Certificates

You will need a certificate as proof of a valid marriage in many of the proceedings described in this book. Here's where to get it.

Canada	Address	Fee
Alberta	Director, Division of Vital Statistics 9815 Jasper Avenue Edmonton, Alberta	$2.00
British Columbia	Director, Division of Vital Statistics Parliament Buildings Victoria, B.C.	2.00
Manitoba	Recorder, Division of Vital Statistics Department of Health and Social Services 104-401 York Avenue Winnipeg, Manitoba	2.00
New Brunswick	Registrar General of Vital Statistics Department of Health and Welfare Fredericton, New Brunswick	2.00
Newfoundland	Registrar, Vital Statistics Division Department of Health Confederation Building St. John's, Newfoundland	2.00
Nova Scotia	Deputy Registrar General P.O. Box 157 Halifax, Nova Scotia	2.00

Ontario	Office of the Registrar General Macdonald Block Parliament Buildings Toronto, Ontario	3.00
Prince Edward Island	Vital Statistics P.O. Box 3000 Charlottetown, Prince Edward Island	2.00
Quebec	Registrar Department of Health, Family and Social Services Quebec, P.Q.	2.00
Saskatchewan	Director of Vital Statistics Department of Public Health Provincial Health Building Regina, Saskatchewan	2.00
Northwest Territories	Deputy Registrar General of Vital Statistics Yellowknife, N.W.T.	2.00
Yukon	Deputy Registrar General of Vital Statistics Whitehorse, Yukon	2.00

United States of America

Alabama	Registrar of Vital Statistics Alabama Department of Health State Office Building Montgomery, Alabama	$2.00
Alaska	Bureau of Vital Statistics Department of Health and Welfare Pouch "H" Juneau, Alaska, 99801	2.00
Arizona	Clerk of the Superior Court in County where license was issued	Varies
Arkansas	Bureau of Vital Statistics State Department of Health Little Rock, Arkansas, 72201	2.00
California	Bureau of Vital Statistics, Registration 744 P Street Sacramento, California, 95814	2.00

Colorado	Clerk and Recorder, County Court House, County seat where marriage performed	Varies
Connecticut	State Department of Health Public Health Statistics Section 79 Elm Street Hartford, Connecticut, 06115	1.00
Delaware	Bureau of Vital Statistics State Board of Health Dover, Delaware, 19901	2.00
District of Columbia	Clerk, District of Columbia Court of General Sessions Washington, D.C., 20001	2.00
Florida	Bureau of Vital Statistics State Board of Health P.O. Box 210 Jacksonville, Florida, 32201	2.00
Georgia	County Ordinary, County where license was issued	$2.00
Hawaii	Research and Statistics Office State Department of Health P.O. Box 3378 Honolulu, Hawaii, 96801	2.00
Idaho	Bureau of Vital Statistics Department of Health Boise, Idaho	$1.00
Illinois	County Clerk in County where license was issued	2.00
Indiana	Clerk of the Superior Court in the County where license was issued	Varies
Iowa	Records and Statistics Division Department of Health Des Moines, Iowa, 50319	1.00
Kansas	Division of Vital Statistics Department of Health State Office Building Topeka, Kansas, 66612	2.00
Kentucky	Records since July 1st, 1958: Office of Vital Statistics State Department of Health 275 East Main Street	2.00

	Frankfort, Kentucky, 40601	
	Prior to July 1st, 1958:	Varies
	Clerk of the County Court in	
	County where license was issued	
Louisiana	Except New Orleans:	2.00
	Clerk of the Court in Parish	
	where license was issued	
	New Orleans:	2.00
	Bureau of Vital Statistics	
	City Health Department	
	1 W 03	
	City Hall	
	Civic Centre	
	New Orleans, Louisiana, 70112	
Maine	Office of Vital Statistics	1.00
	State Department of Health	
	State House	
	Augusta, Maine, 04330	
Maryland	Division of Vital Records	2.00
	State Department of Health	
	State Office Building	
	301 W. Preston Street	
	Baltimore, Maryland, 21201	
Massachusetts	Registrar of Vital Statistics	1.00
	272 State House	
	Boston, Massachusetts, 02133	
Michigan	Vital Records Section	2.00
	Department of Health	
	Lansing, Michigan	
Minnesota	Clerk of District Court in	2.00
	County where license was issued	
Mississippi	Division of Public Health	2.00
	and Statistics	
	Board of Health	
	P.O. Box 1700	
	Jackson, Mississippi, 39205	
Missouri	Recorder of Deeds in County	Varies
	where license was issued	
Montana	Division of Records	1.00
	and Statistics	
	State Department of Health	
	Helena, Montana, 59601	

Nebraska	Bureau of Vital Statistics Department of Health Lincoln, Nebraska, 68509	2.00
Nevada	County Recorder in County where license was issued	Varies
New Hampshire	Bureau of Vital Statistics Department of Health and Welfare Division of Public Health 61 South Spring Street Concord, New Hampshire, 03301	1.00
New Jersey	State Registrar of Vital Statistics Department of Health P.O. Box 1540 Trenton, New Jersey, 08625	$2.00
New Mexico	County Clerk in County where marriage was performed	Varies
New York	Except New York City: Office of Vital Records State Department of Health Albany, New York, 12208	2.00
	New York City: Borough in which license was issued	3.00
	Bronx: 1780 Grand Concourse Bronx, New York, 10457	3.00
	Brooklyn: Municipal Building Brooklyn, New York, 11201	3.00
	Manhattan: Municipal Building New York, New York, 10007	3.00
	Queens: Office of City Clerk 120-55 Queen's Boulevard Borough Hall Station Jamaica, New York, 11424	3.00
	Richmond: Borough Hall St. George Staten Island New York, 10301	3.00

161

North Carolina	Since January 1st, 1962: Public Health Statistics Section State Board of Health P.O. Box 2091 Raleigh, North Carolina, 27602	1.00
	Prior to January 1st, 1962: Registrar of Deeds in County where marriage was performed	Varies
North Dakota	County Judge in County where license was issued	2.00
Ohio	Probate Judge in County where license was issued	1.00
Oklahoma	Clerk of the Court in the County where the license was issued	Varies
Oregon	State Board of Health Vital Statistics Section P.O. Box 231 Portland, Oregon, 97207	2.00
Pennsylvania	County Court House in the County seat where the license was issued	3.00
Rhode Island	Division of Vital Statistics Room 351 State Office Building Providence, Rhode Island, 02903	1.00
South Carolina	Since July 1st, 1950: Bureau of Vital Statistics Board of Health Sims Building Columbia, South Carolina, 29201	1.00
	Prior to July 1st, 1950: Probate Judge in County where license was issued	1.00
South Dakota	Division of Public Health Statistics Department of Health Pierre, South Dakota, 57501	2.00
Tennessee	Division of Vital Statistics Department of Public Health Cordell Hull Building Nashville, Tennessee, 37219	2.00

Texas	County Clerk in County where license was issued	Varies
Utah	County Clerk in County where license was issued	Varies
Vermont	Bureau of Vital Statistics Office of Secretary of State Montpelier, Vermont, 05602	1.50
Virginia	Bureau of Vital Records and Health Statistics State Department of Health James Madison Building P.O. Box 1000 Richmond, Virginia, 23208	1.00
Washington	Since January 1st, 1968: Bureau of Vital Statistics Department of Health 313 Public Health Building Olympia, Washington, 98501	2.00
	Prior to January 1st, 1968: County Auditor of the County where license was issued	2.00
West Virginia	County Clerk in County where license was issued	Varies
Wisconsin	Bureau of Health Statistics Wisconsin Division of Health P.O. Box 309 Madison, Wisconsin, 53701	2.00
Wyoming	Division of Vital Statistics State Department of Public Health Cheyenne, Wyoming, 82001	2.00

United Kingdom

England	General Register Office Somerset House London, W. C. 2	72 ½ new pence
Scotland	General Register Office New Register House Edinburgh, Scotland	72 ½ new pence
Northern Ireland	General Register Office Fermanagh House Ormeau Avenue Belfast 2, Northern Ireland	72 ½ new pence

Note

You can always obtain a marriage certificate for any foreign country by writing to the nearest embassy or consulate, giving the necessary information and waiting a hell of a long time. The sensible way to do it, avoiding bureaucratic delay and expense, is to write to a relative or friend in that country, and ask him to get the certificate for you.

Appendix D

Table of Equivalent Statutes

	Custody	Family Court	Maintenance of Parents	Maintenance of Children	Protection and Adoption of Children
ALTA.	Domestic Relations Act	Family Court Act; Domestic Relations Act	Maintenance Orders Act	Maintenance Orders Act	Child Welfare Act
B.C.	Equal Guardianship of Infants Act	Wives' and Children's Maintenance Act; Provincial Court Act	Parents' Maintenance Act	Wives' and Children's Maintenance Act	Protection of Children Act
MAN.	Child Welfare Act	Wives' and Children's Maintenance Act	Parents' Maintenance Act	Child Welfare Act	Child Welfare Act
N.B.	Habeas Corpus Act	Deserted Wives' and Children's Maintenance Act	Parents' Maintenance Act	Deserted Wives' and Children's Maintenance Act	Child Welfare Act
NFLD.	Family Courts Act	Maintenance Act; Family Courts Act	Maintenance Act	Maintenance Act	Child Welfare Act
N.S.	Infant's Custody Act	Wives' and Children's Maintenance Act; Family Court Act	Parents' Maintenance Act	Children's Maintenance Act	Child Welfare Act
ONT.	Infant's Act	Deserted Wives' and Children's Maintenance Act; Provincial Courts Act	Parents' Maintenance Act	Children's Maintenance Act	Child Welfare Act
P.E.I.	Judicature Act	Children's Act	Children's Act	Children's Act	Children's Protection Act
QUE.	Civil Code 200	Civil Code 165, 169, 170	Civil Code 166-7	Civil Code	Youth Protection Act; Adoption Act
SASK.	Infant's Act	Deserted Wives' and Children's Maintenance Act	Parents' Maintenance Act		Child Welfare Act

	Sale of Jointly Owned Lands	Title or Possession of Matrimonial Property	Marriage	Alimony and Maintenance	Enforcement of Orders for Maintenance or Alimony in Family Court
ALTA.	Devolution of Real Property Act	Married Women's Act	Marriage Act	Domestic Relations Act	Family Court Act
B.C.	Partition Act	Married Women's Property Act	Marriage Act	Divorce and Matrimonial Causes Act	Provincial Court Act
MAN.	Real Property Act	Married Women's Property Act	Marriage Act	Court of Queen's Bench Act; Divorce and Matrimonial Causes Act	Wives' and Children's Maintenance Act; Child Welfare Act
N.B.	Devolution of Estates Act	Married Women's Property Act	Marriage Act	Divorce Courts Act	Juvenile Courts Act; County Magistrate's Act
NFLD.	Judicature Act	Married Women's Property Act	Solemnization of Marriage Act		Family Courts Act
N.S.	Partition Act	Married Women's Property Act; Married Women's Deeds Act	Marriage Act	Alimony Act	Family Court Act
ONT.	Partition Act	Married Women's Property Act	Marriage Act	Matrimonial Causes Act	Provincial Courts Act
P.E.I.	Real Property Act; Chancery Act	Married Women's Property Act	Marriage Act	Divorce Courts Act	Children's Act
QUE.	Civil Code 623, 689-693, 696-8, 700, 711		Civil Code (many sections)		
SASK.	Devolution of Real Property Act	Married Women's Property Act	Marriage Act	Matrimonial Causes Act; Queen's Bench Act	Deserted Wives' and Children's Maintenance Act

	Enforcement of Orders made in other provinces	*Registration of Maintenance Order against Land*
ALTA.	Reciprocal Enforcement of Maintenance Orders Act	Maintenance Orders Act
B.C.	Reciprocal Enforcement of Maintenance Orders Act	Order 409, Sec. 12
MAN.	Reciprocal Enforcement of Maintenance Orders Act	Judgments Act
N.B.	Reciprocal Enforcement of Maintenance Orders Act	
NFLD.	Maintenance Orders (Enforcement) Act	
N.S.	Maintenance Orders Enforcement Act	
ONT.	Reciprocal Enforcement of Maintenance Orders Act	Judicature Act (alimony order only)
P.E.I.	Reciprocal Enforcement of Maintenance Orders Act	Children's Act
QUE.	Reciprocal Enforcement of Maintenance Orders Act	
SASK.	Maintenance Orders Act	Deserted Wives' and Children's Maintenance Act